ASHE Higher Education Report: Volume 34, Number 4
Kelly Ward, Lisa E. Wolf-Wendel, Series Editors

Intellectual Property in the Information Age: Knowledge as Commodity and Its Legal Implications for Higher Education

Jeffrey C. Sun

Benjamin Baez

2763343328

Intellectual Property in the Information Age: Knowledge as Commodity and Its Legal Implications for Higher Education
Jeffrey C. Sun and Benjamin Baez
ASHE Higher Education Report: Volume 34, Number 4
Kelly Ward, Lisa E. Wolf-Wendel, Series Editors

ISSN 1551-6970   electronic ISSN 1554-6306   ISBN 978-0-4704-7900-1

The ASHE Higher Education Report is part of the Jossey-Bass Higher and Adult Education Series and is published six times a year by Wiley Subscription Services, Inc., A Wiley Company, at Jossey-Bass, 989 Market Street, San Francisco, California 94103-1741.

For subscription information, see the Back Issue/Subscription Order Form in the back of this volume.

CALL FOR PROPOSALS: Prospective authors are strongly encouraged to contact Kelly Ward (kaward@wsu.edu) or Lisa Wolf-Wendel (lwolf@ku.edu). See "About the ASHE Higher Education Report Series" in the back of this volume.

Visit the Jossey-Bass Web site at **www.josseybass.com.**

Printed in the United States of America on acid-free recycled paper.

The ASHE Higher Education Report is indexed in CIJE: Current Index to Journals in Education (ERIC), Current Abstracts (EBSCO), Education Index/Abstracts (H.W. Wilson), ERIC Database (Education Resources Information Center), Higher Education Abstracts (Claremont Graduate University), IBR & IBZ: International Bibliographies of Periodical Literature (K.G. Saur), and Resources in Education (ERIC).

Advisory Board

The ASHE Higher Education Report Series is sponsored by the Association for the Study of Higher Education (ASHE), which provides an editorial advisory board of ASHE members.

Contents

Executive Summary

Intellectual property refers to valued, intangible creations of the mind. The law of intellectual property affords rights associated with the expressions, products, processes, or marks derived from knowledge. Intellectual property can take the form of copyrights for original expressions, patents for inventions and discoveries, trademarks for distinguishing names or symbols, and trade secrets for information held from the public to give an entity a competitive advantage over another person or organization (see Hammersla, 2006).

Why Is Intellectual Property a Critical Issue in Higher Education?

For many years, higher education, an environment critically engaged with intangible objects, has been faced with questions about intellectual property rights (see Kaplin and Lee, 2006). In 2004, *The Chronicle of Higher Education* surveyed ten legal experts to ask them to identify pressing legal issues that would likely emerge in the following five years. Among the common themes, these individuals reported intellectual property as a significant legal concern.

Following the literature and the law, matters concerning intellectual property slowly gained attention in higher education around the 1980s, but more recently, the attention over intellectual property policies and practices in higher education has accelerated and reached a high priority for administrators, faculty, staff, and students at U.S. colleges and universities. In other words, the experts' forecasts in 2004 appear on target, as numerous legal issues have challenged members of the higher education community on the nature and scope of intellectual property since that publication. Moreover, questions regarding intellectual property at colleges and universities do not appear to be waning.

What Drives Changes in the Treatment of Intellectual Property in Higher Education?

Intellectual property has become essential to higher education because of economic, political, and social forces making knowledge and research serve as central commodities to the information age. Because ideas and expressions translate into commodities, the treatment of intellectual property at colleges and universities has changed. Now universities must balance the legal parameters, the various competing interests associated with the intellectual commodities, and the technological advancements that rapidly alter the policies and practices surrounding treatment of these intangible creations and discoveries (Levine and Sun, 2003). Based on a synthesis of the laws and literature of copyrights, patents, trademarks, and trade secrets in higher education, the authors present a model that depicts the environmental pressures (the economic, political, and social forces) and the prevailing factors (the legal parameters, technological advances, and competing interests) that shape intellectual property policies and practices at colleges and universities.

The analyses of the literature and the law in the framework reveal several major impacts on higher education:

The legal parameters to intellectual property foster higher education's commercial and trade-like activities such as commercialization through technology transfer of research, distribution of teaching especially through online media, and licensing of institutional logos. Consequently, higher education's participation increasingly blurs the lines between its public function and private interests.

Once afforded exceptions to the law, educational professionals may no longer maintain special status under intellectual property laws. Instead, the treatment of academic professionals as mere employees appears more prevalent. For example, in the debate about ownership of faculty coursework, one group of authors argues that the materials belong to the institution under the work-for-hire doctrine contained in the Copyright Act. Similarly, a body of literature also discusses the weakening state of the professoriate to control its environment in other instances of intellectual property creations.

An inequity in the law poses potential barriers for faculty and staff at public institutions. The legal conundrum of sovereign immunity drives states to act freely, privatize, and hold themselves not monetarily liable for violations of intellectual property. At the same time, holders of intellectual property may decide to sue individual state employees instead. If that situation occurs, the law may not protect state employees from personal liability for actions based on copyright infringement conducted on behalf of the state, nor can the state use its resources to defend its employees sued for personal liability.

Working within the legal parameters, members of the higher education community recognize the effects of different copyright and patent categories. Depending on the type of copyright or patent, holders of the intellectual property maintain different exclusive rights and duration of protection. Additionally, the form of copyright or patent determines the manner in which the holder might protect or others might legally gain access to use the protected work. Given these parameters, colleges and universities also follow the same logic in their intellectual property policies and practices. In essence, intellectual property policies and practices at colleges and universities are moderated by the type of copyright or patent that one wishes to protect or rightfully use.

Colleges and universities increasingly recognize that a single creation or invention may consist of multiple interests. That is, works may qualify for multiple forms of intellectual property protections, and institutions of higher education may unbundle those rights. For example, a musical performance offers rights over the musical composition, including rights to the music and lyrics, as well as the recording. Similarly, an online course potentially offers bundled rights that colleges and universities may unbundle and identify, which would reflect an institution's intellectual property policies and practices.

For institutions of higher education, the issue of whether to seek intellectual property protections over academic works presents several conflicting positions. On the one hand, proponents of university engagement in patent activities argue that the intellectual property protections ensure proper attribution of the works, allow higher education to facilitate scientific progress over industry, typically maintain inventors' interests, and generally serve the public interest. On the other hand, opponents of university engagement in patent activities argue that the limited monopoly is counter to the institution's role of public service, creates data blockages such as withholding information and keeping data secret, shifts the focus more toward applied rather than basic research, contributes to licensing approval problems with patent thickets, and passes greater costs to the end user, the consuming public.

While colleges and universities engage in commodifying knowledge, they also express frustration and challenges associated with seeking access to copyrighted and patented works. Because of confusion about the legal parameters regarding fair use, researchers report "pedagogical costs" and "distribution hurdles" that serve as impediments to the educational environment. Similarly, layers of patents, also known as patent thickets, make use of certain products and processes difficult.

Colleges and universities are expected to implement social controls to curb peer-to-peer network exchanges of pirated works (see, for example, von Lohmann, 2007). Many institutions of higher education engaged in activities that educated their community—providing educational seminars and notices, actively policing their campus network and warning potential pirates to cease and desist, and using sophisticated software to monitor network activities—before the 2008 Reauthorization of Higher Education Act mandated them.

Simply put, these highlights of institutional policies and practices illustrate how intellectual property enables and disables the higher education community.

What Is the Future of Intellectual Property for Higher Education?

Colleges and universities grapple with very complex legal questions requiring them to identify and address what intellectual property is, who can own the products of knowledge, and how to manage the various legal, technical, and competing interests associated with intellectual property. Although an underlying issue is whether anyone *should* own ideas or expressions, the information society has clearly accepted the basic premise of ownership over knowledge. Ownership necessarily privatizes ideas and expressions and makes them inaccessible to others. That postsecondary institutions and their faculty, which traditionally have served the public function of creating and disseminating knowledge as well as preparing citizens for participation in civic life, can own ideas, make a profit from those ideas, and, more significantly, withhold public access to those ideas, leads to questioning their public functions and the role they play in a democratic society. It also questions how institutions of higher education can participate in the environment of commodifying knowledge (McSherry, 2001). The movement toward creating intellectual property regimes is strong, and so the arguments associated with privatizing knowledge will continue. Members of the higher education community, especially administrators, should understand these arguments and how to respond to them.

Foreword

As knowledge production takes new and different forms, intellectual property concerns are of increasing interest to faculty and administrators in higher education. Given the growth in intellectual property activity, campuses need to define and address the topic forthrightly. The role of intellectual property in higher education has shifted considerably, requiring campuses to focus directly on intellectual property as part of research administration and legal protection. Yet information about the shifting terrain of knowledge production and proliferation is limited. Jeffrey Sun and Ben Baez, in *Intellectual Property in the Information Age: Knowledge as Commodity and Its Legal Implications for Higher Education,* have not only filled a knowledge gap but also astutely synthesized and analyzed existing information, both literature and case law, and presented it in a way that is useful and interesting.

The monograph covers the gamut with regard to intellectual property. The authors provide an informative overview of what intellectual property means and the types of activity it encompasses. Too often, intellectual property is a topic of academic banter, but the specifics and definition of the banter are not always clear, making it easy to talk about a complex issue in a superficial way. The monograph is a great resource for those seasoned and experienced with issues associated with intellectual property as well as those who may be less familiar with all that intellectual property entails. The authors provide a framework for looking at intellectual property by examining the nuances of political, social, and economic forces as well as detailed information about and examples of the different manifestations of intellectual property and the application of related law.

In an era when technology makes it easy for knowledge to transcend traditional academic boundaries, the information in this monograph is sure to be of use for faculty and students engaging in knowledge production as well as the administrators who govern such activity. Given the increasingly entrepreneurial nature of higher education where faculty members, students, and institutions are encouraged to be creative with the development of new ideas, concerns associated with intellectual property are here to stay. The authors not only provide solid background on what intellectual property means but also do an excellent job of examining the origins and applications of legal issues associated with copyright, patents, trademarks, trade secrets, and how the law is and has been applied to these outcomes of intellectual property. Given the connections of intellectual property with entrepreneurialism in higher education, this monograph makes a good companion to the upcoming ASHE monograph on entrepreneurial domains authored by Matthew Mars and Amy Metcalfe.

This monograph is a must-read for faculty, staff, students, and administrators interested in intellectual property and associated legal issues. Readers will find information relevant for the development and application of policy to govern matters associated with intellectual property, and they will find information about associated practices and examples from different campuses. In addition, readers with a research orientation will find a compendium of relevant literature and case law that is a rare find in one resource. There is much to learn about intellectual property, and this monograph is sure to become the go-to resource on the topic.

Kelly Ward
Series Editor

 Published online in Wiley InterScience
(www.interscience.wiley.com) • DOI: 10.1002/aehe.3405

Overview of Intellectual Property

INTELLECTUAL PROPERTY REFERS to the intangible items that typically produce or create products, processes, expressions, marks, or nonpublic information. Derived from the U.S. Constitution, "intellectual property law provides a personal property interest in work of the mind" (O'Connor, 1991, p. 598). Two prevailing justifications support intellectual property: (1) a utilitarian bargain between the creator and society in which the former is granted a limited monopoly in return for disclosure and circulation of the intellectual work and (2) a Lockean justification in which property rights inhere to deserving creators entitled to the fruits of their labor (Munzer, 1990; Ostergard, 1998). This monograph addresses these two justifications from a framework that contextualizes the discussion around the role of the economic, political, and social forces that contribute to intellectual property policies and practices in the higher education community, and, more directly, this monograph examines college and university intellectual property policies and practices that are largely shaped from existing legal parameters, technological advancements, and competing interests.

Factoring these multiple considerations, intellectual property rights involve trade-offs in public policy. Specifically, they are intended to achieve an appropriate balance between incentives to innovate and diffusion of new knowledge, such that the economic costs of granting the right do not outweigh the benefits of increased innovation (Wallerstein, Mogee, and Schoen, 1993). The argument most commonly advanced for intellectual property rights is that absent the laws, free-riders will consume the intellectual works without fair contribution for the costs associated with the works. Consequently, the free-riders contribute to a market failure. Viewed another way, without intellectual property rights, markets fail to function properly because society fails to provide sufficient incentives to induce socially optimal amounts of investment in public goods in the form of new scientific and technological knowledge (David, 1993).

To explore these ideas, this monograph examines in great detail two kinds of intellectual property: copyrights and patents. Though we recognize the significance of trademarks and trade secrets, we focus primarily on copyrights and patents in this monograph because they represent the most significant issues in higher education in the information age. Emphasizing these forms of intellectual property, this monograph frames the rights derived from legal parameters pertaining to intellectual property, technological advancements, and competing interests from various actors involved. Naturally, we use many legal concepts in this monograph, but we minimize legal jargon and attempt to make this information accessible to the lay, albeit educated, audience. But two legal definitions are useful here. *Infringement* means the violation of a legally recognized right and generally is used to refer to violations of most forms of intellectual property. *Piracy* is a form of infringement and typically refers to the unauthorized copying of copyrighted works (Wallerstein, Mogee, and Schoen, 1993). Given these definitions, we recognize that the role of intellectual property policies and practices in higher education institutions includes finding ways to balance multiple goals: to create incentives for innovation, protect interests in inventions and discoveries, and legally comply with appropriate uses of protected works (Munzer, 1990; Ostergard, 1998). Keeping these goals in mind, we present a framework to examine intellectual property policies and practices in higher education institutions.

The Framework

Economic, political, and social forces largely shape intellectual property policies and practices at colleges and universities, much like other policies and practices in higher education (see, e.g., Altbach, Berdahl, and Gumport, 2005; Ficsor, 2006). Although each force by itself plays a role in shaping colleges' and universities' policies and practices toward intellectual property, collectively these forces represent the larger environmental conditions that affect the legal parameters, technological advancements, and competing interests that shape the policies and practices surrounding treatment of these intangible creations and discoveries in higher education. To elaborate further on the forces and prevailing factors that contribute to the intellectual property policies and practices at colleges and universities, we now discuss each component of our framework.

Forces

Intellectual property has become essential to higher education because of economic, political, and social forces making knowledge and research serve as central commodities of the "information age." Because ideas and expressions translate into commodities, the environmental pressure over the treatment of intellectual property at colleges and universities changed. Accordingly, we briefly explain how the information age altered the treatment of intellectual property along with the corresponding policies and practices in higher education.

Economic Forces. Current economic trends make consideration of intellectual property imperative to the broader understanding of the forces that shape the treatment of creations and discoveries derived in and from institutions of higher education. The increasing importance of intellectual property is largely attributable to the shift that moved the United States and other nation-states from an industrial society to an "information society." "Information society" refers to economies in which control over knowledge has replaced control over matter as the ultimate source of economic power (May, 2000; see also Benjamin, 2003).

Intellectual property is essential to economies based on information or knowledge (Hettinger, 1989). In the information age, ideas and expressions become commodities, and universities must contend with the legal parameters, the various competing interests associated with the intellectual commodities, and the technological advancements that rapidly alter the policies and practices surrounding treatment of these intangible creations and discoveries.

Today the economic health of nations and corporations is determined largely by their ability to develop, commercialize, and exploit scientific and technological innovations; intellectual property rights are the legal means by which one can protect one's investment in innovation (Wallerstein, Mogee, and Schoen, 1993). As organizations use knowledge as the catalyst to increase the values of their products and services, they seek to capture such knowledge for their exclusive control. Knowledge, once feeding the productive processes and services of these corporations, now is itself deemed property. Once knowledge is deemed property, intellectual property laws become central to the economy (May, 2000). In other words, intellectual property is the legal form of the information age (Boyle, 1997).

Not surprisingly, the complexities of dealing with intellectual property in the information age have become more pressing in higher education. Indeed, in 2004 legal experts identified intellectual property as one of the most pressing issues facing higher education ("Pressing Legal Issues," 2004). Simply put, with the shift from an industrial to an information economy, higher education now operates under a different context, one in which colleges and universities regularly contend with numerous legal questions about the nature and scope of intellectual property (see, for example, Crews, 1993; Dutton, 2002; Katz, 1998).

Political Forces. At the same time, laws and policies reward innovation. These political structures form the national priorities that stimulate innovation and define intellectual property rights (Mowery, Nelson, Sampat, and Ziedonis, 2001; Nelson, 2001). In fact, the United States maintains a national system of innovation that places colleges and universities at the forefront as participants that harvest discoveries and creations, even with (or perhaps because of) federal research dollars. For instance, in 1980 the federal government uniformly permitted colleges and universities to seek and own patents for products or processes invented with federal research dollars. This shift in policy redirected intellectual property policies and practices in higher education, and that movement persists today.

Pursuant to the political agenda of the national system of innovation, this information economy has and continues to transform the role of universities; the most decisive change has been technology transfer from the university to industry (Miyoshi, 2000). "Technology transfer" is a term that represents the activities universities engage in to move their research to the market. Slaughter and Leslie (1997) argue that postindustrial, transnational capitalism uses higher education no longer for the primary purpose of training workers, as technology makes industrial workers less necessary, and that the political-economic environment has emphasized more research and development activities. Consequently, intellectual property has become extremely important to universities because the intellectual property of universities plays a crucial role in political-economic exchanges, and potential revenues generated from intellectual property allow universities to rely less on government support.[1] Universities have thus become active players in the intellectual property scene, seemingly transforming themselves from knowledge producers for the public good into intellectual property producers for themselves and for-profit firms (Baez, 2005). These events represent the political forces.

Furthermore, given the economic forces making intellectual property imperative to economic wealth, universities become implicated in controversies specifically addressed to the United States as a nation-state. For example, international protection of intellectual property rights is premised on a U.S. notion of property ownership and legal entitlements. The protection of intellectual property, as Aoki (1998) pointed out, is replicated on a global scale when U.S. law is taken as a model, and to the extent international agreements provide rights to information, they undermine traditional territorial and political notions of sovereignty. As these international policies grow in international scale, they, by their presence, impact the intellectual property policies and practices of U.S.-based colleges and universities, particularly those institutions with a transnational presence.

Social Forces. Intellectual property rights, particularly during the information age, purportedly address what is usually understood as the "public good problem." That is, given that the cost of creation is high but the cost of reproduction is low and that once the work is created it may be easily reproduced without depleting the original creation, intellectual property protection is necessary to ensure that the creator has an economic incentive to create works that, at least ultimately, will benefit the public (Litman, 1990). Consequently, because technology makes creations initially expensive but expansive and reproduction easy at a substantially lower cost, the legal history of intellectual properties in the United States has been one of access and use, balanced with incentives and rewards.

Stated differently, in the United States, the government grants intellectual property rights primarily to promote the public interest, such as creating a balance between the economic benefits to the inventor and the interests of society at large (Wallerstein, Mogee, and Schoen, 1993). To promote the welfare of the public, intellectual property rights establish an incentive structure through laws and policies that reward the holder of the intellectual property. This protection is critical for institutions, including higher education institutions, as the discoveries and creations contribute to the public good in the form of solutions to societal problems.

Intellectual property rights are deemed to protect investments in innovation by granting the owner a temporary, limited monopoly on the use of the innovation. Because the owner can keep the economic benefits of the innovation, being able to keep the economic rewards serves as further incentive for others to innovate, further benefiting the public through more creations and discoveries in the market. Of course, intellectual property rights also restrict the public from using the innovation without permission, and they prevent others from developing and improving on innovations, thus limiting the benefits to the public (Wallerstein, Mogee, and Schoen, 1993). Given these considerations, the social forces shape the extent to which intellectual property policies and practices at colleges and universities serve the public good.

Direct Factors

While the social, political, and economic forces change the role of intellectual property in colleges and universities, these forces also shape, and are shaped by, three primary factors that directly contribute to intellectual property policies and practices at colleges and universities: the legal parameters, new technologies, and competing interests (see, for example, Jobe, 2006; Levine and Sun, 2003; Monaghan, 2006; Powell and Owen-Smith, 1998).

Legal Parameters. The laws pertaining to intellectual property rights serve as the starting point for policies and practices in higher education regarding the rights governing creations and discoveries. Although intellectual property laws themselves serve as the most obvious example, laws governing contracts, state employment relations, sovereign immunity, and international treaties at times also establish the parameters for intellectual property policies and practices at colleges and universities. For example, under copyright law, the default rule indicates that the author holds the ownership rights to expressions; however, contract law permits the author to negotiate the ownership rights with another party. As such, the legal parameters extend beyond intellectual property laws and touch on other laws that contribute to the language of institutions' intellectual property policies and practices.

Technological Advancements. Technological advancements contribute to the language of intellectual property policies and practices at colleges and universities. For example, current electronic technologies enable delivery of courses online. Online courses represent expressions of content that qualify today for intellectual property protection, primarily because, unlike traditional courses, they can be "fixed" onto a tangible form as required by copyright laws. Consequently, because of technological advances, teaching online qualifies for copyright protection and affects intellectual property policies and practices in institutions of higher education (Levine and Sun, 2003; Salomon, 1999).

Competing Interests. Because intellectual property law establishes ownership and control over the works, competing interests from various individuals and groups also contribute to the crafting of intellectual property policies and practices in higher education (Bobbitt, 2006; Daniel and Pauken, 1999). For example, when ownership over online courses emerged as a central question in higher education, the interests of institutions, students, and faculty emerged (Levine and Sun, 2003). As competing interests came to light, colleges and universities responded with intellectual property policies and practices (see Figure 1).

Impact on Core Academic Functions

As legal parameters, new technologies, and competing interests contribute to the formation of intellectual property policies and practices at colleges and universities, we recognize the impacts of the policies and practices in the core academic functions of colleges and universities, particularly in terms of teaching and research activities. As we noted earlier, online courses qualify for

FIGURE 1
**Forces and Factors that Contribute to Intellectual Property
Policies and Practices in Institutions of Higher Education**

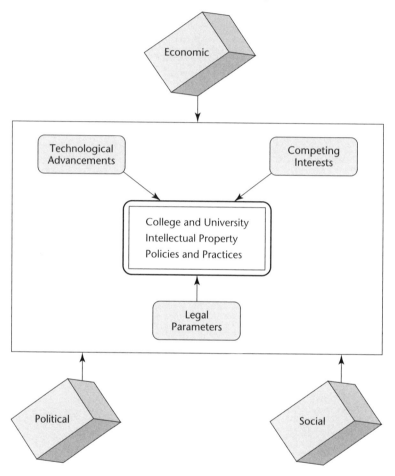

copyright protection. Because copyright law has been extended, more or less problematically, into the instructional function of higher education, colleges and universities have been faced with concerns about ownership rights of faculty handbooks or explicit agreements between parties, with rights and privileges associated with modifying online courses (that is, derivative works), with approaches to using existing copyrightable works through online courses, and with other special arrangements such as unbundling rights when multiple rights are associated with the creation of one course (see, for example, Daniel and Pauken, 1999; Kelley, Bonner, McMichael, and Pomea, 2002).

Like teaching, intellectual property also affects research. For example, once discoveries of DNA sequences qualified as patentable knowledge, a slew of possible patentable research associated with living matter became commodities in the information age (see, for example, Blumenstyk, 2005). As such, today patent law raises questions about what is patentable and thus shapes the course of research in more or less explicit ways. Again, competing interests in these "properties" interfere in the traditional functions of institutions of higher education in ways previously unimagined.

Colleges and universities grapple with very complex legal questions requiring them to identify and address what is intellectual property, who can own the products of knowledge, and how to manage the various legal, technical, and competing interests associated with intellectual property. We consider several complex questions in this monograph: If a professor creates a database of research findings, who holds the proprietary rights to those data? If academic researchers gather data on a patient's DNA coding, can they patent that knowledge? If professors design an online course, who holds the copyright? When students download pirated music and movies from peer-to-peer networks from a college server, can the college be held liable? If an accounting professor records her lectures and sells the digital recordings to a professional development training company, will the college win a suit over ownership rights against the company and the professor? If a student takes copious notes and sells them to a company that distributes course notes and if the professor in that course sues the company for copyright infringement, will she prevail?

Intellectual property policies and practices in higher education certainly affect the academic core. Universities can dictate the terms of intellectual property rights for faculty and students (through employment contracts and policies related to academic programs). The question of ownership of patents is generally moot, as universities have claimed such ownership for some time through state legislation and preemployment contracts. Furthermore, individuals who have contested university ownership usually have not prevailed (Baez and Slaughter, 2001). Universities have not pursued copyrights for traditional academic work such as publications and course materials (but today, new technologies create controversy over ownership of online course materials). Even with publications, the question seems generally moot as well, as faculty members usually assign their rights to a publisher, which then owns the copyrighted materials. The issue as to whether anyone *should* own ideas, however, raises philosophical concerns, such as whether *ideas* or expressions of ideas should be owned. This question has significant political implications as well. All ownership necessarily privatizes ideas and makes them inaccessible to others. That postsecondary institutions and their faculty, which traditionally have served the public function of creating and disseminating knowledge as well as preparing citizens for participation in civic life, can own ideas, make a profit from those ideas, and, more significantly, withhold public access to those ideas, leads to questioning their public functions and the role they play in a democratic society (McSherry, 2001).

This monograph explores these overarching concerns and the corresponding issues along with others through an examination of the laws (as primary sources) and scholarly and research literature. The monograph frames its analysis along two dimensions: (1) the economic, political, and social forces that shape and are shaped by (2) more direct, prevailing factors of legal parameters, new technologies, and competing interests that contribute to the intellectual property policies and practices at colleges and universities. This framework guides the discussion of the intellectual property in the information age. Thus, we offer an overview of the monograph to illustrate the development of key intellectual property concepts and its application of the framework.

Organization of the Monograph

This chapter presents a framework for understanding the role of intellectual property in the field of higher education. In particular, this framework accounts for the economic, political, and social factors, which set the stage for the roles of law, technology, and competing interests. Based on the literature and legal analyses, these dimensions represent identifiable yet also interrelated components to account for intellectual property subject matter, the rationale for its protection, and, in particular, how the higher education community tackles the issues of these property rights during this information age. To structure our overarching framework, this chapter presents the arguments and evidence of the current economic, political, and social factors that contribute to the growing importance of knowledge and information and the corresponding value on intellectual property. It also addresses the role of laws as legal parameters that guide current practices and policies in higher education. In addition, it reveals the nature and impact of technological advancements onto our intellectual property practices and policies in higher education. Equally important, it raises questions about various competing interests from parties directly and indirectly connected with intellectual property works. In other words, it offers the framework that structures this monograph.

Following the model, the next chapter presents the general concepts of federal copyright law, including copyright subject matter, duration of the protection, rights granted under the protection, and ownership determinations. This coverage raises several questions: Who owns the copyrighted works of faculty publications and course lectures as well as the works of students and staff? How does the Internet change conceptions of copyrighted works in higher education? In what ways might higher education reenvision copyright protections to unbundle the works similar to musical works, which contain rights associated with musical composition, lyrics, performance, and sound recordings?

"Copyright and Fair Use" lays out the concepts of fair use in terms of laws and guidelines established with industries that control many copyrighted works. Our discussion asks what qualifies as fair use, emphasizing the differences among books, music, television broadcasts, and video recordings; how technologies such as peer-to-peer software, photocopy machines, and learning management systems (for example, Blackboard) altered concepts of fair use; and how various groups have expressed their interests in protecting or gaining access to copyrighted works through fair use and how institutions of higher education have responded.

"The Law of Patents" introduces basic concepts about federal patent law as applied to higher education. In particular, the chapter describes types of patents, subject matter of patents, filing requirements, and the ownership and rights associated with federal patent protections. The chapter raises numerous questions: What qualifies for patent protections? How do the nature and scope of patent coverage change with emerging discoveries, particularly in the biotechnology field? What struggles exist between and among groups over use of patentable materials for research, instruction, and other academic purposes?

"Patents and Higher Education's Entry into the Market" traces the development of patent activities in higher education and discusses the issues surrounding the debate about university patents. The chapter presents questions about what laws and federal policies contributed to university patent activities; how technological advancements such as nanotechnology spurred on new inventions and discoveries and altered the landscape for colleges and universities; and how inventors and universities balanced questions about access, control, and attribution of the patented works.

Building on earlier chapters, "Shared and Related Concerns About Intellectual Property" describes additional legal topics covering shared and related concerns with copyright and patent laws. Specifically, it addresses topics of trademarks, trade secrets, international treaties governing intellectual property, and sovereign immunity. The chapter raises questions: With the growing presence of transnational universities, how do universities respond to the international treaties pertaining to intellectual property in light of their emphases on trade? How has the ease of mimicking college logos and identifying unauthorized users of logos, particularly with new electronic technologies, altered enforcement policies and practices in higher education? How do expressions of universities' and corporate partners' interests with preliminary discoveries and confidential formulas affect intellectual property policies at colleges and universities?

Finally, the conclusion revisits our framework that identifies the forces and direct factors contributing to the language of intellectual property policies and practices in institutions of higher education. Drawing on previous discussions from the preceding five chapters, the chapter illustrates how the economic, political, and social forces shape the treatment of intellectual property as well as the policies and practices at colleges and universities. In addition, we further explain the relationship among legal parameters, which include laws specifically about intellectual property as well as laws related to intellectual property, technological advancements, and competing interests as direct factors that contribute to intellectual property policies and practices in institutions of higher education.

The Law of Copyrights

IN THEIR MEDIEVAL ORIGINS, copyrights had nothing to do with the encouragement of intellectual creativity or originality of expression. The rights to published works remained legally unprotected until the fifteenth century, when the printing press made the rewards for publishing or plagiarism far greater than ever before. The new technology of printing transformed the copying business by substantially increasing the disparity between the cost of the first copy and the cost of subsequent copies. In other words, the economics of publication shaped copyright law more than the economics of authorship (David, 1993).

The first known copyrights appeared in Renaissance Italy, which granted monopolies in the form of exclusive licenses to print or sell books for a particular term, prohibitions of the importation of books abroad, and patents for improvement of printing and typography. The rights of the author were disregarded because much of the demand was for already existing books, like the Bible, which was in the public domain and whose authors (along with several generations of heirs) were likely long dead and not inquiring about rights (David, 1993).

The modern right to the author's copyright in the United States occurred in the eighteenth century, which limited the exclusive right to printing new materials to fourteen years and gave holders of copyrights for existing books the sole right to print for twenty-one years. Specifically, in the United States the constitutional basis for intellectual property derives from Article I, §8, cl. 8: "Congress shall have Power . . . to promote the progress of science and useful arts, by securing for limited times to authors and inventors the exclusive right to their respective writings and discoveries." As an incentive to foster original, creative works, the law grants exclusivity over the expression. In practice the law protects the owner of the right from such events as unauthorized use, dissemination, and alteration of one's work. At the most basic level, the federal copyright law grants authors a limited, exclusive right to their writings. As Justice O'Connor acknowledged in the majority opinion for *Harper & Row Publishers, Inc.* v. *Nation Enterprises* (1985), "[t]he Framers intended copyright itself to be the engine of free expression. By establishing a marketable right to the use of one's expression, copyright supplies the economic incentive to create and [to] disseminate ideas" (1985, p. 558). Consequently, the provisions under the law provide for exclusivity over a period of time as an incentive to foster creative works.

Copyright Law

Framed around the economic, political, and social forces, incentives furthered the goals of intellectual property creations. Additionally, other more direct factors—more specifically, legal parameters, competing interests from various actors, and technological advancements—present new creations or alter the way creations are treated at colleges and universities. Accordingly, in light of the legal parameters surrounding creative works, technological advancements, and various actors (individuals and groups) vying for property interests, this chapter responds to these overarching questions regarding copyright in higher education: What are original expressions? Who owns them, if one even knows? What rights are derived from this ownership and others' use? In the form of copyright policies and practices, how has the higher education community responded to these questions of ownership and usage of original expressions?

Copyright Qualifications

Under the federal act, a copyrightable item is an original expression that is fixed in some tangible format. The general language of the statute states in relevant part that copyrightable products are the "original works of authorship fixed in any tangible medium of expression, now known or later developed, from which they can be perceived, reproduced, or otherwise communicated, either directly or with the aid of a machine or device" (17 U.S.C. §102(a)). Viewed another way, the determination of whether an expression is copyrightable has two major components: originality and fixation of the work.

Originality is a fundamental element in copyright law. In fact, the U.S. Supreme Court stated in *Feist Publications, Inc.* v. *Rural Telephone Service Co., Inc.* (1991) that "originality remains the *sine qua non* of copyright" (p. 348). Consequently, without originality, copyright would not be codified. For a product to qualify as an original expression, it must meet the requirements of independence and creativity. Independence refers to the free thought process of the product. That is, the expression cannot be copied from another source. Likewise, the creativity standard requires that the expression be something different and not imitated, but it does not need to be novel or unique. The creativity requirement maintains a very low threshold; it must simply have some small amount of creativity. For example, in a case filed by the University of Minnesota to assert its rights over statements used in a psychometric instrument (that is, survey items), the court determined that the survey items met the originality standard and constituted copyrightable matter (*Applied Innovations, Inc.* v. *Regents of the University of Minnesota* (1989)). Put simply, originality is a basic component for copyrightable works, and as the Court in *Feist* (1991) indicated, "Originality does not signify novelty; a work may be original even though it closely resembles other works so long as the similarity is fortuitous, not the result of copying" (p. 345).

Besides the originality component, the expression must be fixed through some tangible form of expression.[2] According to the federal copyright law, fixation of an expression occurs "when its embodiment in a copy or phonorecord, by or under the authority of the author, is sufficiently permanent or stable to permit it to be perceived, reproduced, or otherwise communicated for a period of more than transitory duration" (17 U.S.C. §101). For instance, as the Court acknowledged in *U.S.* v. *Board of Trustees of the University of Alabama* (1997), a doctoral student's printed dissertation, study abstract, and drafts of the dissertation met the requirements of having originally authored works, which are fixed on tangible media of expression. Additionally, courts have recognized other fixed forms of original work, including video game images *(Williams Electronics, Inc.* v. *Artic Intern., Inc.* (1982)) and broadcasts that are simultaneously recorded *(Baltimore Orioles, Inc.* v. *Major League Baseball Players Association* (1986)).

In sum, to qualify for copyright, the general principles require the works to meet the standards of originality and fixation on any tangible medium of expression. Furthermore, copyright covers the expressions, but they do not protect the ideas themselves. For example, a publication is copyrightable, but the ideas about a publication concept do not qualify for copyright protection. In other words, copyright protects the actual works themselves, not the ideas.

Copyright Subject Matter

Copyrightable works come in multiple forms such as symbols, words, or pictures. Initially, when the federal copyright law was enacted in 1790, copyrightable products were limited to maps, charts, and books. As new technologies emerged along with the shift in economic, political, and social priorities, various actors placed pressure on Congress to protect other forms of expression like motion picture and sound recording studios. Today, the copyright law enumerates eight categories of copyrightable subject matter: (1) literary works; (2) musical works, including any accompanying words; (3) dramatic works, including any accompanying music; (4) pantomimes and choreographic works; (5) pictorial, graphic, and sculptural works; (6) motion pictures and other audiovisual works; (7) sound recordings; and (8) architectural works (17 U.S.C. §101 (2008)). Based on the copyright subject matter category, different rights and privileges attach, such as the forms that constitute an expression, different uses (or exclusive rights) associated with each category, legal anomalies framed around artistic and societal benefits, and the length of the copyright protection. Thus, the type of copyright affects the nature and scope of the protection.

As a general rule, a copyrighted work is an expression that falls into one of the eight categories. In terms of volume, the most common form of copyrightable items produced in higher education falls under "literary works." According to the federal statute, literary works "are works, other than audiovisual works, expressed in words, numbers, or other verbal or numerical symbols or indicia, regardless of the nature of the material objects" (17 U.S.C. §101 (2008)). Literary works may be "books, periodicals, manuscripts, phonorecords, film, tapes, disks, or cards, in which they are embodied" (17 U.S.C. §101 (2008)). In addition, the courts declared that literary works may be represented as journals (*Salinger* v. *Random House, Inc.* (1987); *Wright* v. *Warner Books, Inc.* (1991)), letters (*Wright* v. *Warner Books, Inc.* (1991)), a song's lyrics (*Zomba Enterprises, Inc.* v. *Panorama Records, Inc.* (2007)), brochures (*Edmark Industries* v. *South Asia International* (2000)), computer programs (*Apple Computer, Inc.* v. *Franklin Computer Corp.* (1983)), exam questions (*National Conference of Bar Examiners* v. *Multi Legal Studies, Inc.* (1980, 1982)), greeting cards (*Roth Greeting Cards* v. *United Card Company*, (1970)), and survey items used to construct a test or measures such as a psychometric instrument (*Applied Innovations, Inc.* v. *Regents of the University of Minnesota* (1989)).

Although literary works represent the largest copyrightable category in higher education, technology has the capacity to transform the formats of existing copyrightable works to new and additional copyrightable formats (Arewa, 2006; Townsend, 2003). For instance, written lectures, articles, dissertations, play manuscripts, and lyrics may appear as expressions in the forms of podcast lectures, online articles, digital dissertations, videocast plays, and digitally recorded songs. That transformation to a different format (for example, podcast lectures, online articles, digital dissertations, videocast plays, and digitally recorded songs) potentially unbundles the final works into multiple copyrights for various interested parties. To understand this concept of unbundling of copyright protections from a final work, one might examine the copyrights associated with musical works for illustrative purposes.

Musical works may be unbundled just like online classes, videocast plays, and online articles. Generally speaking, "musical works" refers to the melody, harmony, rhythm, and structure of the music, which may include lyrics or accompanying words. In practice, musical works appear in the form of songs, orchestral scores, operas, and even advertising jingles. The treatment of musical works and the related components, however, is not straightforward, because a musical performance potentially involves numerous interested parties with different roles. Accordingly, the law separates the various interests associated with copyrighted music. According to *Staggers* v. *Real Authentic Sound* (1999), "Copyright protection extends to two distinct aspects of music: (1) the musical composition, which is itself usually composed of two distinct aspects—music and lyrics; and (2) the physical embodiment of a particular performance of the musical composition, usually in the form of a master recording" (p. 61).

A brief discussion about copyright protection associated with a song illustrates these various rights. Under copyright law, the songwriter may copyright the lyrics, which are categorized as literary works. The lyrics, even without any accompanying music, retain copyright protection. In addition, the musical expression, which contains four components (melody, harmony, rhythm, and structure), qualifies for copyright protection under musical works, and the musical expression may also include the words (Autry, 2002). Furthermore, the recording of the musical performance, whether with or without words, typically occurs on a phonorecord such as a CD, which constitutes a sound recording and is covered under a separate category of the copyright law (see below). In sum, similar to works created with new technologies, copyright over musical works contains multiple rights that may be unbundled.

Because multiple actors (for example, artists, musicians, recording studios, record producers, and distributors) participate in the process of musical works from the creative act to the technical responsibilities, the law delineates the different rights associated with the various works (for example, literary works, musical works, and sound recordings) that contribute to the overall output to the end user. This concept of unbundling rights for various actors could be applied to higher education (Kelley, Bonner, McMichael, and Pomea, 2002; see also Carnevale and Young, 1999). For example, to move a lecture into an online interactive course typically involves multiple parties such as the instructor as composer and performer, the course designer and other technology support staff as producers, and the university as recording studio and distributor. Although the current legal arrangements do follow this structure of unbundling rights, the potential for such negotiated rights is available under the law, and these enumerated categories play a significant role in enabling an arrangement to unbundle legal rights such as contracts for copyrighting academic services.

The categories of copyrightable subject matter also point out the legal anomalies. Although much of the copyright law balances economic, political, and social conditions, selected portions of the law are framed solely around artistic and societal benefits, and their statutory language responds to the moral rights connected with the works. For example, to protect the interests of artists and society from loss of limited pieces of art, the Visual Artists Rights Act adds additional protection to authors of visual arts (17 U.S.C. §106A (2008)). A visual art covers a single "still photographic image produced for exhibition purposes only"; a painting, drawing, print, or sculpture; or a limited edition of those items with two hundred or fewer copies that are consecutively numbered and contain the author's signature to properly attribute the work (17 U.S.C. §101). Under this law, authors of visual arts have a right of attribution to the work. In other words, the author is given proper credit for the work regardless of whether the visual art is sold or passed on to another person.

In addition, the author of the visual art may disclaim authorship to the work if it is distorted, mutilated, or modified in a manner that "would be prejudicial to his or her honor or reputation" (17 U.S.C. §106A(a)(2) (2008)). Moreover, the law extends rights to the visual art's continuation. Specifically, the author can prevent intentional distortion, mutilation, or modification of the work as well as intentional or gross negligence to works of recognized stature.[3] Violation of any of these provisions constitutes copyright infringement. Consequently, because the nature of the rights (that is, protecting the integrity of the works, attribution to the author, and the continuation of visual art of a recognized stature) is associated with the author of the work, the law attaches these rights only to the author. As a result, the rights are not transferable, although the author can waive rights established under the Visual Artists Rights Act. In short, distinguishable from other copyrightable subject matter, which provides exclusive rights to the copyright owner or holder, works of visual art attach exclusive rights to the author of the work. Practically speaking, if a visual art qualifies under the Visual Artists Rights Act, its use may be so restricted that it cannot be displayed for an online class—even if the artist is a professor at the institution—without expressed authorization of the artist. Similarly, under the statutory language, digital images likely do not qualify for the special rights contained in the Visual Artists Rights Act. Simply put, the law protects the artist and the artwork, but it does not adequately afford educational access to the art.

Finally, the copyrightable subject matter determines the length of the copyright protection. In fact, besides the subject matter consideration, the term period of copyright protection also depends on when the work became published (if at all) and by whom (see Hirtle, 2008). As a general rule, works published after 1977 with some type of notice maintain federal copyright protection for the life of the author plus seventy years. If the author is a corporation, the copyright protection lasts for ninety-five years from publication. The complication associated with the calculation of the copyright protection term reflects the multiple categories of work and the various iterations of the law, which are products of the economic, political, and social forces driven by special interests (for example, the Sonny Bono Term Extension Act).

Rights of Copyright Protection

Assuming qualification of copyrightable subject matter, the copyright holder retains a set of protections to the work's exclusive use in terms of controls over reproduction, adaptation, distribution, performance, and display rights. In other words, the copyright holder may freely duplicate the work, modify the work such as converting its format or deleting portions, disseminate copies of the work, perform the work (that is, "recite, render, play, dance, or act" through some mechanism such as video recording), or display the work (for example, in the form of an image or artwork). In addition, copyright holders of sound recordings may perform the work for digital audio transmission (17 U.S.C. §106). The next chapter discusses the fair use of copyrighted works along with the conditions and limitations connected with those uses.

Copyrights and Faculty, Students, and Staff

As we established in the previous chapter, the information age advanced the value of intellectual property as a critical commodity in society. Given that focus, the ownership of intellectual property emerges to the forefront. According to the federal copyright law, the legal presumption attaches ownership to the author unless the work is transferred to another party or the work was conducted under some contractual or employment arrangement (17 U.S.C. §§101, 201). The latter exception (that is, whether the work was conducted under some contractual or employment arrangement) represents a highly debated and contentious issue to determine the treatment of ownership rights of works made by faculty, students, and staff. Ultimately, the context of the authored work becomes an important determination. To explore the significance of context as a determinant for copyright ownership, we examine the law as a primary source to set the legal parameters and the literature as a secondary source to explain the arguments based on both technological advancements and actor-based interests over faculty scholarly and creative works, faculty course materials (especially in light of distance education), student works, and staff works.

Faculty Scholarship

Absent some expressed agreement to the contrary, some universities and scholars interpret professors' participation in research as a job function (Denicola, 2006; Simon, 1983; Wadley and Brown, 1999). Under this viewpoint, the copyright ownership resides with the university. Specifically, the "work made for hire" provision of the copyright law effectively transfers the ownership of a work from the author to the entity that has paid for her or his services (17 U.S.C. §201(b)). In the case of a professor's work, the most frequently asserted argument to support the interests of the institution is that the professor is under a work-for-hire agreement (see "Faculty Course Materials" below for a more extensive discussion of this doctrine). According to the Copyright Act, works made for hire occur when "the employer or other person for whom the work was prepared is considered the author[,] unless the parties have expressly agreed otherwise in a written instrument signed by them, [that the employer] owns all of the rights comprised in the copyright" (17 U.S.C. §201). Stated differently, under this logic the professor is hired to engage in scholarly research. Therefore, the work is for the institution, and the institution holds rights of ownership. The institution may also waive its rights to the scholarship as per academic custom and permit the faculty member to keep the copyright.[4] Nevertheless, under the work-for-hire argument, by default the college or university retains the rights.

Absent an expressed agreement to demonstrate a work-for-hire arrangement, the legal and educational research literature overwhelmingly concludes that copyright ownership over faculty scholarship resides with the faculty author (see, for example, Borow, 1998; Dreyfuss, 1987; Kilby, 1995; Kulkarni, 1995;

Meyer, 1998). Two frequent arguments surface in support of the proposition that professors own the copyright to their scholarship. One argument is that the conditions of the work-made-for-hire provision are not met with professors' work on research, so it does not apply to that context. Several legal commentators have asserted that the copyright law defaults ownership rights to the author, and because the work-made-for-hire provision is not applicable to faculty, the default rule applies (Borow, 1998; Kilby, 1995; Meyer, 1998). According to these scholars, the work-made-for-hire provision requires the employer to maintain direction, control, and supervision over the works (Borow, 1998; Kilby, 1995). They argued that although universities may require faculty to publish or participate in research, universities do not dictate, direct, control, and supervise faculty research in part because that would violate academic freedom as well as academic norms. Furthermore, Kilby (1995) pointed out that academic scholarship contributes to the field of study, not the employing university, and so the university's role of not directing, dictating, and supervising the research is consistent with the expectation of a noncopyright owner.

Another argument takes a constitutional interpretation. The scholars with this perspective analyzed the constitutional source for intellectual property law and indicated that the law's basis stems from a reward-incentive concept to the creator or the motivating force of the work (Borow, 1998; Dreyfuss, 1987; Kilby, 1995; Meyer, 1998). Because universities are neither the creator nor the motivating force, the intellectual property of professors' research (for example, academic papers and scholarly presentations) and creative activities (for example, artwork or musical composition) cannot reside with the university or any other random party unless expressly transferred. According to Meyer (1998), giving the university copyright ownership, when it is neither the creator nor the motivating force, would only create unjust enrichment, a legal term used to signify an unfair benefit to another party.

In sum, the literature overwhelmingly supports the proposition that faculty own and control their scholarship. Most often, writers assert one of two reasons to support this conclusion. One rationale is that faculty scholarship does not constitute work made for hire because institutions have little input in professors' research projects that qualify for copyright protection. Furthermore, colleges and universities typically do not direct, control, and supervise the works. Another rationale is that the institutions do not serve as the motivating force for the work's creation. Therefore, the institution does not retain ownership of faculty works. These reasons serve as viable arguments to grant copyright ownership of faculty research; however, these reasons represent highly contested arguments over ownership to faculty works over course content, especially in terms of online courses, and as discussed later, they are inconsistent with the practice and policies regarding the ownership of faculty's patentable research.

Faculty Course Materials

As indicated, the literature for faculty course materials does not offer a clear interpretation of who owns the copyright. With the increasing number of online courses and the movement toward a more competitive market in higher education, many recognize the potential and possibly inevitable debate surrounding the intellectual property rights attached to recorded classes and other course materials (see, for example, Bobbitt, 2006; Daniel and Pauken, 1999; Lape, 1992; McIsaac and Rowe, 1997; Rhoades, 1998; Scott, 1998; Wadley and Brown, 1999). In particular, this body of literature has focused primarily on whether intellectual property in course content resides with the professor or the institution.

Faculty Ownership of Course Content. A group of authors argue that faculty, not the institution, own course content. As the primary justification for institutional ownership of faculty course content is premised on the copyright law's work-made-for-hire provision, the authors who advance the perspective of faculty owning their course content present three arguments that revolve around the nonapplicability or exception of the work-made-for-hire doctrine.

One argument indicates that the work-made-for-hire provision in the federal law is not applicable to professors (Daniel and Pauken, 1999; Dreyfuss, 1987; Lape, 1992; Kulkarni, 1995; Seeley, 2001). These authors contend that the nature of professors' work does not fit the elements of work made for hire. That is, the work is not commissioned or directed, as the legal provision intends to cover. Instead, professors engage in creative work and work independently, and creativity and independence are what the law specifically intends to promote. Scully (2004) pushes the point further and postulates that "the starting point for restoring the intellectual property balance for copyrighted works of authorship between professors and universities is to recognize that the work of authorship begins with teaching, to which other written and fixed copyrightable formats are derivative, and not the other way round" (p. 265). Thus, if the institution records the instructor, that work is a derivative piece to the lecture. A set of legal commentators forwards another argument that interprets the existence of an academic exception to the work-made-for-hire doctrine (Daniel and Pauken, 1999; Dreyfuss, 1987; Holmes and Levin, 2000; Kulkarni, 1995; Kwall, 2001; Lape, 1992; Scully, 2004). As support for this exception, these commentators cite three cases that discussed this issue. In *Williams* v. *Weisser* (1969), a UCLA professor sued a company, Class Notes, to prevent the dissemination of his lectures and to seek monetary damages. Following common-law and existing California state statutes, the court found in favor of the professor as the owner of his expressions. The court began its analysis with the issue of whether the institution or the professor had held the ownership rights. The court determined that the professor was deemed the author and owner. In distinguishing this employment context with others, the court noted that "university lectures are *sui generis*" (p. 547). That is, they are unique and of their own class; therefore, they should be treated differently from the work of most other kinds of employees. Unfortunately, this case was decided before the last substantial overhaul of the Copyright Act in 1976, so its validity is uncertain.

The second case involved a lawsuit to determine the order of the authors' names for a publication. The court determined that the joint authorship product describing a proposed academic program was to be shared among the authors and not owned by the institution (*Weinstein* v. *University of Illinois* (1987)). The ultimate issue, however, neither was about faculty teaching nor involved a dispute between the faculty and its institution. In a third case, *Hays and MacDonald* v. *Sony Corporation of America* (1988), the court interjected a passing comment—legally referred to as a dictum—that "a college or university does not supervise its faculty in the preparation of academic books or articles, and is poorly equipped to exploit their writings, whether through publication or otherwise" (p. 416). These three cases appear to support the argument that the professors' coursework is unique and thus not subject to the work-made-for-hire doctrine.

A third argument raised in support of faculty ownership of course materials centers on academic custom and tradition, including academic freedom (Holmes and Levin, 2000; Kulkarni, 1995; Kwall, 2001; Lape, 1992; Laughlin, 2000; Scully, 2004). Under this argument, faculty ownership rights follow a long history and tradition in the academic community, a logic that supports the academic exception to the work-made-for-hire doctrine. Per academic custom, faculty have rights to their lectures, handouts, and other course expressions. Equally important, if universities own professors' course works, then derivative works and other materials would be under the institution's direct control and would stifle professors' academic freedom. Faculty may not be able to modify, reproduce, or distribute course materials as they see fit. That unintended but potential consequence would harm society, and, accordingly, academic custom justifies a public policy argument that allows professors to hold the copyright over course materials they create. Furthermore, as Holmes and Levin (2000) note, professors change universities, so if universities owned the course materials, professors would be denied the freedom to take their materials with them.

Institutional Ownership of Course Content. Proponents of the position that the respective institution owns the faculty-created course content base their arguments primarily on the work-made-for-hire doctrine. Drawing from language contained in the Copyright Act, the work-made-for-hire doctrine indicates that any work produced during employment constitutes ownership to the institution (Barnett, 2001; Klein, 2004; Packard, 2002; Rothman, 2007; Simon, 1983). According to the Copyright Act, works made for hire occur when the employer or someone who commissions the work is considered the author and is entitled to the copyright unless the parties agree otherwise (17 U.S.C. §201). With course materials and instruction, like the arguments asserted over university ownership of research, the university would assert that the professor is hired to create these materials and thus the university owns them.

Indeed, Simon (1983) argued that a reading of the 1976 Copyright Act's language inevitably places the work of faculty members under the work-for-hire doctrine and specific language suggesting this ownership delineation is not necessary. He reached the conclusion that the statutory language should not exempt faculty from the work-made-for-hire doctrine. Furthermore, in *Community for Creative Non-Violence* v. *Reid* (1989), the U.S. Supreme Court made it clear that "work prepared by an employee within the scope of his or her employment" (p. 738) constitutes work made for hire. To determine whether the work occurred in the scope of employment, the Court examined the rules governing the law of agency.[5] In analyses from several legal commentators, professors as employees meet the work-made-for-hire standards articulated in the statute as well as explanations given in the case law.

Besides the applicability of the work-for-hire doctrine, authors who support ownership of faculty-created work for the institution refute claims that the doctrine does not apply to or contains exceptions for professors' course materials. For instance, in response to the claims of an academic exception to the work-made-for-hire doctrine, several scholars have analyzed the legislative history of the Copyright Act of 1976 as well as the case law since the law was passed (for example, Barnett, 2001; Klein, 2004; Packard, 2002; Townsend, 2003). Based on their legal interpretations, "academic exception has not survived the revisions to the Copyright Act" and the cases do not stand for the proposition that the academic exception is alive in the case law (Klein, 2004, pp. 168–169). The work-made-for-hire doctrine still determines the copyright ownership of course materials, and that ownership resides with the employing university absent a signed contract stating transference of rights. That universities do not often attempt to capture the products of teaching is more a matter of custom than of law.

Similarly, in opposition to the argument that academic custom trumps the work-made-for-hire doctrine, several authors vigorously dispute that assertion (Klein, 2004; Packard, 2002; Rothman, 2007). For example, Rothman (2007) presents reasons why analysis of professional custom would improperly influence and negatively affect copyright law in educational settings, arguing that academic custom arguments negate the autonomy and freedom for parties to contract. Furthermore, custom creates expectations even when they would be unfair or unjust. Consequently, Rothman counters the notion that the academic custom argument could (or should) be asserted. Packard (2002) also indicates that although academic freedom might have been the one strong argument to justify professors' copyright ownership, institutional academic freedom appears to overcome individual academic freedom arguments. Thus, the academic custom assertion should fail.

Institutional Policies. Some have recommended reliance on institutional policies to dictate ownership (Kwall, 2001; Laughlin, 2000; Packard, 2002; Scully, 2004). Indeed, recommendations inform the scholarly and practice communities on policy content and construction, particularly because they examine the presence of copyright policies (Bobbitt, 2006; Kelley, Bonner, McMichael, and Pomea, 2002; Lape, 1992; Loggie and others, 2006, 2007; Sanders and Richardson, 2002; Sanders and Shepherd, 2000), the terms and conditions of the policies (Bobbitt, 2006; Kelley, Bonner, McMichael, and Pomea, 2002; Lape, 1992; Loggie and others, 2006, 2007; McIsaac & Rowe, 1997; Sanders and Richardson, 2002; Sanders and Shepherd, 2000), and the dynamics of the policy construction and adoption processes (Myers, 2003; Welsh, 2000; Zhang and Carr-Chellman, 2006). Unfortunately, the debate continues and the literature offers no definitive determination as to whether the faculty or the institution own faculty-created course content absent an expressed agreement.

Alternatively, the statutory provisions indicate that if a work-made-for-hire arrangement exists, then absent a signed agreement the ownership remains with the employer. Therefore, the initial legal determination—which is currently an open question—is whether faculty work on course materials falls under the work-made-for-hire doctrine. To circumvent this legal debate, an expressed contract with signatures from both a university agent and the professor could eliminate any challenges between the parties, and several legal commentators recommend that contracts be executed for every university employee (Borow, 1998; Kilby, 1995).

Summary. In sum, the law offers little guidance to set parameters for institutions to establish policies and practices, yet to construct an institutional policy, faculty and administrators at a given college or university must respond to the following questions: Are faculty course materials work made for hire? If so, is there an exception for academics and teachers? If not, is there a signed agreement transferring the copyright ownership to the faculty (or any other party)? Put simply, the discussion above presents the copyright ownership dilemma for professors' course materials and illustrates how legal parameters, technological advancements, and actor-based interests can play a role in intellectual property policies and practices at institutions of higher education.

Student and Staff Works

The copyright ownership of students' works typically resides with the student (Todd, 2007; Townsend, 2003). That general rule may change, however, with joint work with faculty (Patel, 1996; Todd, 2007), a determination that the student worked as an employee (Patel, 1996; Seymore, 2006a, 2006b), or substantial funding and expressed arrangements of institutional ownership *(Iowa State Univ. Research Foundation, Inc.* v. *American Broadcasting Company, Inc.* (1980)). Cases that emerge under these circumstances typically conclude that the university owns the copyrighted works. But the analysis becomes muddled again in the context of students who serve in the capacity of instructors or teaching assistants. That determination, particularly as more students serve as instructors or teaching assistants for online courses, will likely follow one of two possible approaches. First, the court would simply follow a similar legal analysis to that of determining the copyright ownership of faculty course materials. Or second, the court would follow the logic that the student-instructor or teaching assistant prepares the course materials for the learning process, and so those expressions are akin to a student's paper or supervised project. Regardless of which approach the courts take, the determination of copyright ownership of students' works as an instructor or teaching assistant is uncertain.

By contrast, the debate about copyright ownership is less controversial for nonacademic staff (see, for example, *Foraste* v. *Brown Univ.* (2003)). For instance, in a case regarding a staff member's work, the plaintiff, Foraste, sued for copyright ownership over the photographs he took as a university staff photographer. In relevant part, the university policy indicated that unless otherwise agreed upon, university employees retained copyright ownership of their works; however, the court, relying on the Copyright Act and several other cases for statutory interpretation, clearly indicated that the university photographer conducted his work under a work-made-for-hire arrangement. Under the federal law, when the copyrighted work constitutes work made for hire, an organizational policy is insufficient for the employer to surrender its rights to the work. In other words, under a work-for-hire arrangement such as the court recognized with assignments for university staff, the university legally gives up ownership and other rights with a signed, expressed agreement. Because one did not exist, the court indicated the university photographer's works fell under the work-made-for-hire doctrine, but the court noted in the case's facts that Foraste was not employed in any capacity as faculty. Therefore, by inference, an argument might be made that the matter would have been different if Foraste held a faculty appointment and the pictures pertained to that role. Because the facts of the case pertained only to the university, the ruling supports only the legal proposition that works of nonacademic staff involve work made for hire and that ownership thus resides with the employer unless a signed agreement indicates otherwise.

Chapter Summary

This chapter presents general concepts of copyright, with particular emphasis on determination of the work's author, subject matter, term, exclusive rights, and ownership. Addressing these legal constructs, copyright law touches on matters related to the author's integrity, attribution, rewards, and control over the works (for example, use, reproduction, alteration, distribution, display) (Levine and Sun, 2003). These interests in copyrights derive from economic, political, and social forces that explain the complicated categories of copyrightable subject matter and the terms for copyright protection. Indeed, the copyright law creates the various copyright subject matter categories with the intent to "unbundle" rights. For instance, a musical work does not represent a single copyright. Instead, the law factors the multiple parties, who have an interest in the musical work, and it gives copyright protection over the musical composition, lyrics, performance, and sound recording. Despite these great efforts from industry to parse out a variety of rights and litigants, surprisingly the analyses of copyright ownership and rights in higher education establish a dichotomy between the institution and faculty, students, or staff. Kelley, Bonner, McMichael, and Pomea (2002) suggest, however, that it is time to unbundle the interests and rights of the multiple authors and situations involved in works of the higher education community, particularly to account for differing legal rights, technological advancements, and various competing interests.

Finally, Scully (2004) raises a provocative claim: "Perhaps the timing is now right to rethink copyright for academic authors, taking into account a global, binary coded world, where no authorial expression survives without virtually instantaneous duplication, manipulation and reuse" (p. 276). If future technology eventually takes place with instantaneous activity, works typically copyrighted may no longer qualify. For instance, online courses are fixed to a medium of expression through delivery over the Internet, which qualifies them for copyright protection; however, a live lecture of a class in a brick-and-mortar classroom does not qualify for copyright protection because it is not fixed to a medium of expression. Therefore, with technological advancements, course materials may one day transmit instantaneously without any fixation. In other words, technology, which created a greater need for copyright protection especially over course materials, may one day create environments in which course materials may no longer qualify for copyright protection as the law is currently constructed. Consequently, Congress and others will need to reframe copyright concepts to prepare the legal terrain for the future.

Copyright and Fair Use

THIS CHAPTER FOCUSES on the use of copyrighted works. As a general rule, users of copyrighted work may license selected works for a fee through a centralized licensing service such as Copyright Clearance Center for articles and books, icopyright.com for Web sites, American Society of Composers, Authors and Publishers for musical works and lyrics, the Motion Picture Licensing Corporation for motion picture studios, and Artists Rights Society for visual arts. Nevertheless, given certain conditions, the law on fair use permits limited access of copyrighted works. Because the educational enterprise relies heavily on fair use of copyrighted works, this chapter defines areas of fair use, articulates the legal conditions and limitations of fair use, describes the confusion surrounding qualifications of fair use materials, identifies the various parties who have a financial interest in fair use, and highlights obstacles to fair use when heightening commercial values are associated with the copyrighted works.

Fair Use

The law permits limited uses and reproduction of copyrighted materials without the owners' permission. We refer to it as "fair use." The copyright law permits "fair use" of works after weighing four factors:

1. The purpose and character of the use, including whether such use is of commercial nature or is for nonprofit educational purposes;
2. The nature of the copyrighted work;

3. The amount and substantiality of the portion used in relation to the copyrighted work as a whole; and

4. The effect of the use upon the potential market for or value of the copyrighted work [Copyright Act, 17 U.S.C. §107 (2008)].

The statute indicates that acceptable fair use purposes may include "criticism, comment, news reporting, teaching (including multiple copies for classroom use), scholarship, or research" (17 U.S.C. §107 (2008)). Indeed, to some extent the law accommodates educational institutions, and, not surprisingly, colleges and universities frequently assert fair use claims of copyrighted works for classroom discussions, readings, display, and demonstrations.

According to Frazier (1999), "Fair use exists in copyright law because there always has been a compelling interest in a democratic society to balance the exclusive rights of publishers with legitimate needs of the public for reasonable and affordable access to information" (p. 1321). Despite this policy interest, the law is not written in a manner that clearly delineates the democratic interests of society and the rights of the copyright holders. Although the law is well settled that copying an entire copyrighted work for profit-making motives fails to adhere to fair use standards (*Zomba Enterprises, Inc.* v. *Panorama Records, Inc.* (2007)), confusion, misinterpretation, and general unawareness of educational users' rights to copyrighted materials still exist (Crews, 1993; Fisher, 1988; Hobbs, Jaszi, and Aufderheide, 2007). In practice, what do the four factors mentioned above really mean?

Fisher (1988) asserted that the lack of clarity in the fair use doctrine makes it difficult for users of copyrightable works to act in a manner consistent with their rights. Rather than assuming fair use, Fisher suspects that the ambiguous statutory language actually prevents legitimate fair uses of copyrighted works from ever happening. In other words, the confusion actually stifles the exchange of the copyrighted works. In addition, Fisher called for a review of the fair use doctrine so the law would factor in an economic approach with public good preferences. In simplified terms, the public good preferences adjust pricing, availability, or fair use determinations through factors that benefit society such as educational purposes. This approach would in turn give those settings special treatment. Specifically, the law would place academic institutions in a preferential category when it uses copyrighted works for purposes that support societal needs such as taking a copyrighted article and disseminating it for academic research or altering a copyrighted work for scholarly purposes. Despite Fisher's proposed approach, the law is not as generous, and as many report, the fair use provisions are for the most part ambiguous and confusing, particularly for educational institutions that tend to use the materials for the public good.

Books and Periodicals

In anticipation of the ambiguity of the law and based on numerous meetings and negotiations, representatives from the Ad Hoc Committee on Copyright Law Revision, the Authors League of America, and the Association of American Publishers, Inc., issued fair use guidelines for books and periodicals in 1976, when the Copyright Act underwent major revisions (U.S. Copyright Office, 1995). The guidelines included provisions for single copies of these materials for research and teaching, multiple copies for classroom use, and other parameters for fair use of copyrighted books and periodicals. These guidelines were touted as extremely helpful (see, for example, Steinbach, 1989) but also criticized as extremely vague (see, for example, Carroll, 2007; Fisher, 1988).

On the one hand, the guidelines offer more detail, clearer acceptable practices, and explicit prohibitions. Compared with the fair use language in the copyright statute (17 U.S.C. §107 (2008)), the guidelines provide significant clarity for educational fair use of books and periodicals. First, the guidelines provide substantially more detail and parameters for duplicating books and periodicals. For example, the guidelines indicate that educators may copy a book chapter, an article from a journal, a short story, and a paragraph from a newspaper for teaching or research purposes. With the statutory language alone, an educator is left to guess what exactly fair use is. Second, the guidelines also establish general principles for multiple copies of works from books and periodicals. Under §107 of the copyright law, fair use determinations factor the "amount and substantiality" of the work, but the provision offers no guidelines on what constitutes an appropriate amount and a substantial portion of a work. Instead, when making multiple copies of a copyrighted work for a class, the guidelines inquire into three factors to determine fair use: degree of brevity, extent of spontaneity, and amount used relative to the cumulative effect. For example, the guidelines indicate that fair use applies if a complete article consists of fewer than twenty-five hundred words, if the decision to use the article occurred without sufficient time to seek copyright permission, and if no more than three articles were copied from the same periodical volume. Third, the guidelines establish which acts and purposes are prohibited. For example, copying shall not serve to circumvent copyright law by displacing books and other copyrighted materials, nor shall fair use apply to consumable materials such as workbooks and standardized tests or involve direct charges to the students for these educational materials.

On the other hand, the guidelines convey mixed messages about limits, still perpetuate levels of ambiguity, and lack legal force. With regard to mixed messages, the guidelines explicitly claim that their purpose is to establish minimum standards for educational fair use, yet they read as maximums. For example, for multiple classroom copies of educational materials, the cumulative cannot be more than "one short poem, article, story, essay . . . nor more than three from the same collective work or periodical volume during one class term" (U.S. Copyright Office, 1995, p. 8). Thus, because the guidelines set upper limits, particularly with regard to the number of articles and words that can be used, they convey maximums despite purporting to offer only minimums as the report indicates.

Not surprisingly, when Crews (1993) reviewed the copyright policies at ninety-eight research universities in the late 1980s to identify their copyright policies, he found that although many adopted the guidelines, they also developed a more restrictive interpretation than necessary. Crews indicated that the guidelines were viewed as limits to avoid litigation. Furthermore, based on interviews with sixty-two educators, media producers, and organizational leaders, Hobbs, Jaszi, and Aufderheide (2007) found that lack of clarity in the fair use guidelines as well as poor communication about these guidelines resulted in the perpetuation of misinformation about the fair use parameters. They noted that those misinterpretations included overly restrictive understandings of the guidelines.

Moreover, with regard to ambiguity, the guidelines basically caution educators that these guidelines represent acceptable practices at the time of the guidelines' establishment but that, in the future, the scope of educational fair use may be broadened or narrowed. Such ambiguity, especially the indefinite time frame and notice when the scope does actually broaden or narrow, is problematic. Hobbs, Jaszi, and Aufderheide (2007) concluded that the cautious academics who are unaware of the guidelines create "pedagogical costs," which include their using "less effective teaching materials" (p. 16). Finally, the guidelines represent negotiations among several parties; however, they do not carry the force of law (Ebenstein, 1987). Thus, institutions know that even if they follow the guidelines they are not released from future claims of infringement. Alternatively, to avoid the fair use determination, institutions often require the copyright holders' permission, creating what Hobbs, Jaszi, and Aufderheide (2007) call "distribution hurdles," which often complicate, delay, or even result in the work's use becoming impractical (Keyser, 2005), or not used at all.

Music

In 1976, several months after the completion of the guidelines for books and periodicals, a joint effort of several organizations—the Music Publishers' Association of the United States, Inc., the National Music Publishers' Association, Inc., the Music Teachers National Association, the Music Educators National Conference, the National Association of Schools of Music, and the Ad Hoc Committee on Copyright Revision—drafted and endorsed *Guidelines for Educational Uses of Music*. These guidelines resemble the basic structure and process of the guidelines for books and periodicals, but they also contain several distinctive aspects.

The guidelines resemble the guidelines for books and periodicals in a few ways. First, like the guidelines for books and periodicals, the music guidelines detail the statutory provisions of fair use. Under the guidelines, educational fair use of music permits:

Temporary emergency copies of music;

Copies of limited sections of music, but never more than 10 percent of musical works for nonperformance academic purposes;

Editing or simplifying music that does not fundamentally alter the work so long as the educator or institute purchased printed copies of the music;

Single copies of performance recordings for evaluation or rehearsal, such as for grading or practice purposes; and

One duplication of the educator's or institution's sound recording for aural exercises or examinations, with the educator or institution required to retain the copy.

Thus, the general tenor is that a brief portion or section of music constitutes fair use, and copies for instructional purposes within defined parameters are acceptable under the law. Second, both guidelines maintain similar principles, such as minimum fair use standards, not maximums. Like the guidelines for books and periodicals, they read more like prescriptive maximums. Moreover, as expected, both guidelines prohibit reproductions and distributions that circumvent copyright. Third, similar to the guidelines for books and periodicals, the music guidelines carefully construct the language of fair use in a manner that does not impinge on the exclusive rights of certain parties. For instance, under the fair use guideline that allows educators to make one copy of a sound recording for aural exercises or examinations, the fair use application applies only to the music, not the sound recording. This distinction demonstrates the interests of the recording studios in retaining their rights (Crews, 2001). Likewise, the guidelines do not include performance rights connected with the music, which also likely represents the interests of certain copyright holders.

The music guidelines also contain several distinctive features compared with the guidelines for books and periodicals. First, although both guidelines articulate more details relative to the statutory provisions for fair use, the music guidelines do not prescribe as many quantifiable levels. Part of the distinction may reside with distinctions between printed materials (that is, books and periodicals) versus music; however, a portion of the distinction may also relate to the policy goal of avoiding overprescription. A second distinction relates to the commentaries surrounding this guideline. Unlike the guidelines for books and periodicals, the section of the music guidelines in the U.S. Copyright Office's Circular 21 (1995) explicitly mentions the disagreements and criticisms associated with the music guidelines by the American Association of University Professors and the Association of American Law Schools. Their disapprovals represent differing interests and perspectives. According to the commentary in the circular, these organizations noted that the guidelines were "too restrictive with respect to classroom situations at the university and graduate level" (pp. 9–10). In other words, both education-based professional organizations assert high "pedagogical costs" with the adoption of the music guidelines. Furthermore, music professors convey problems with the guidelines, particularly use of sound recordings and their need for band, instrumental, and music instruction (see, for example, Woody, 1994).

Television Broadcast Recordings

In 1979, several years after adoption of the guidelines for books and periodicals and music and the technological advances of videocassette recorders, another group with interests in television broadcasts convened a series of meetings to negotiate fair use guidelines. By 1981, this group produced *Guidelines for Off-Air Recording of Broadcast Programming for Educational Purposes*. Generally speaking, the policy permits educational institutions (or educators) to record television broadcasts for instructional purposes for later off-air viewing. The guidelines' basic parameters state that educators cannot record more than one broadcast program or alter the recorded broadcast (although the entire broadcast does not need to be shown). In addition, educators may retain the recording for up to forty-five days and make a limited number of copies within the scope of the educators' legitimate needs. Finally, the television broadcast must display the copyright notice as displayed on the broadcast.

Fair Use Challenge to Course Materials: Course Packs

Course packs are compilations of readings, typically of copyrighted works. They challenge the concepts of fair use for institutions of higher education and the copy centers that faculty use to create course readers (Metcalfe, Diaz, and Wagoner, 2003). Many course packs appear to comply with the copyright law's four factors for fair use as follows. First, the purpose and character of course packs are for nonprofit educational use. Second, the nature of the copyrighted work offers educational knowledge and resources. Third, the amount and substantiality of a copyrighted work is often limited to an article or a book chapter because course packs generally originate from multiple sources. A reading compilation is akin to an edited textbook, however, so a course pack is likely to fail the fourth fair use factor: "the effect of the use upon the potential market for or value of the copyrighted work" (17 U.S.C. §107). That is, the course pack diminishes the chances of students' buying the original work. Course packs also fail to comply with the explicit prohibitions contained in *Agreement on Guidelines for Classroom Copying in Not-For-Profit Educational Institutions with Respect to Books and Periodicals.* Specifically, course packs are created as compilations of readings, and although instructors are likely to use the same readings in subsequent terms, the ultimate legal determination rests on the market impact of selling course packs without copyright permission (*Basic Books, Inc. v. Kinko's Graphics Corp.* (1991); *Princeton Univ. Press v. Michigan Document Servs., Inc.* (1996)).

The push for a market analysis to determine fair use, even within the higher education context, is becoming more pervasive. Metcalfe, Diaz, and Wagoner (2003) examine several scenarios in which higher education asserts fair use of copyrighted materials for purposes such as copies for classroom instruction and research. With each scenario, they identify four frames to present the interests of the creators and public regarding the fair use of copyrighted materials. Specifically, they frame each scenario around the creator or public's interests within an academic frame, technological frame, social frame, and market frame. For example, in a scenario of fair use of copyrighted materials for class, an academic frame examines the instructor's role by assigning the materials; a technological frame views technological resources that host or enable distribution of the materials; a social frame views the overall benefit to the students and society more generally; and the market frame examines the interest of the copyright holders. The interests in the copyrighted materials expressed through the four frames demonstrate the multiple purposes that claimed, fair use materials have to higher education. More important, Metcalfe, Diaz, and Wagoner's frames capture how the recent fair use cases reflect the market frame at the expense of the academic, social, and technological frames.

Several fair use cases arose over copyright infringements from the creation of course packs. The initial course pack case took place in 1982 against New York University. The copy center at NYU reproduced course readers without copyright permission and charged students for the cost of the photocopies. As a result, nine publishers sued NYU. After several months of discussions and negotiations, NYU settled with the publishers, crafted a model copyright policy, distributed a notice of copyright compliance and liability, and sought copyright clearance for subsequent course packs (Bartow, 1998; Crews, 1993, 2001; Steinbach, 1989). According to Crews (1993) and Steinbach (1989), after this case arose many colleges and universities reviewed or instituted a policy on the use, including fair use, of copyrighted works.

Nearly a decade later, several major publishers sued Kinko's, a national photocopy chain, for copyright infringement based on the duplication and distribution of course packs. The suit targeted two Kinko's locations that reproduced course packs for students at New York University, the New School for Social Research, and Columbia University. Kinko's principal argument relied on fair use for educational purpose. The company even asserted that "the evidence shows that course packets are of tremendous importance to teaching and learning, and are the subject of widespread and extensive use in schools throughout the country" and that a ruling inconsistent with fair use "would pose a serious threat to teaching and the welfare of education" (*Basic Books, Inc.* v. *Kinko's Graphics Corp.* (1991), p. 1535). Not persuaded by the fair use and other alternative arguments, the court found Kinko's course packs did not satisfy the fair use exception and that the commercial value of the packets represented duplication of the publishers' works. In short, the court found Kinko's liable for copyright infringement.

Similarly, in 1996, three publishers sued Michigan Document Services (MDS), a commercial copy shop that reproduced course packs for students at the University of Michigan. Like the Kinko's case, MDS defended itself against the infringement claim by asserting educational fair use. The trial court ruled in favor of the publishers, so MDS appealed. Upon the initial appeal, the court overturned the trial court's decision and ruled in favor of the copy shop; however, in the rehearing, thirteen judges of the U.S. Court of Appeals for the Sixth Circuit reviewed the case. Eight judges joined the majority opinion that a market existed for the work, that the works were altered to make a new compilation, and that the guidelines on books and periodicals had some legally persuasive value to determine whether the works qualified as fair use. Five judges dissented, arguing that under the plain meaning of fair use law, MDS was only carrying out what the Michigan professors gathered for the students' educational benefit. Their analysis also pointed out flaws in the majority's assertion of market effects. MDS did not create a market, and the publishers did not plan to enter the market of publishing these readers. Instead, the professors created the readers, and no harm associated with the market effect argument was demonstrated. In short, the dissent raised arguments that the law pertaining to educational fair use appears to extend beyond the strict meaning of the statutory provisions.

The collective effects from the Kinko's and MDS rulings demonstrate several critical points about the fair use of copyrighted materials. First, guidelines such as the *Agreement on Guidelines for Classroom Copying in Not-For-Profit Educational Institutions with Respect to Books and Periodicals* clearly play some role in judicial decisions. The courts appear to use the guidelines as interpretative law. Second, the courts liberally interpreted the market effect factor to discount fair use. The court focused on the market value for readers and the market effects from loss of royalties or sales of anthologies and compilations, even though the publishers would not compile these readings. Because educators would not distribute multiple copies of a set of articles, the compilation into a reader translates into royalty losses for publishers (Rife and Hart-Davidson, 2006). Oddly enough, if the publishers themselves decided to create anthologies based on these professors' course syllabi, they would need copyright permission because the syllabi represent fixed media of expression. Furthermore, because five of the thirteen judges disagreed with the majority opinion in the Michigan case, the market factors argument might not survive in future legal challenges, particularly with new library reserve systems and learning systems management tools that permit instructors to post articles and book chapters for students to review if the library already maintains the collection of readings. Third, for now, these cases narrow the scope in which professors may assert fair use for multiple classroom copies. In light of these decisions, an outside vendor will not reproduce the copies. Furthermore, students cannot purchase the copies from an on-campus duplicating center. Given these circumstances, the university or the professor must pay for the copies themselves by using university equipment. The multiple copies for classroom use, therefore, might be only applicable in departments and institutions with access to copiers and expenses to cover those costs.

Fair Use and Online Instruction

From 1994 to 1997, the Working Group on Intellectual Property Rights in the Electronic Environment (known as CONFU) gathered parties with an interest in copyrights over educational multimedia works to meet at a conference on fair use. During that time, they discussed and negotiated guidelines for educational multimedia, distance learning, digital images, interlibrary loan processes, electronic reserve systems, and computer programs in libraries (Lehman, 1998). Although many provisions were established, the guidelines failed to reach consensus. In fact, many groups expressed disapproval or at least nonendorsement of the guidelines. Only the guidelines that reached consensus and general recognition were published. Some universities, however, including Montclair State University, Piedmont Technical College, the University of Texas, and Washington University, refer to these guidelines in their own guidelines. Because the CONFU policy negotiations failed, lobbyists and many interested parties sought further clarification, and in 2002 Congress passed the TEACH Act, which addresses use of copyrighted materials through digital transmission.

Before 2002, the transmission of educational fair use primarily required a physical classroom and prohibited digital transmissions. At that time, the law prohibited transmission of copyrighted material because the transmission process created another copy, which typically constituted infringement. Criticisms over the legal barriers also pervaded the literature (see, for example, Crews, 2001; Gasaway, 2001b). In response to requests for copyright reform, Congress explored ways to address the legislative hurdles presented to distance education. The legislative policy required the balancing of the copyright holders' interests (for example, authors and publishers) with educators' and students' interests in using copyrighted materials for distance learning (Gasaway, 2001a).

The outcome became the passage of the Technology, Education, and Copyright Harmonization Act of 2002, frequently referred to as the TEACH Act.

The TEACH Act permits educational institutions to use certain copyrighted materials through distance education mediums (see Exhibit 1). Because the TEACH Act balanced the political, economic, and social interests of the copyright holders and those of the educational field in the context of technological media, the law has multiple conditions and qualifications (see, for example, Ashley, 2004; Crews, 2002; Gasaway, 2001a). As several have indicated, the TEACH Act created a set of seemingly onerous limitations and conditions to online fair use (Ashley, 2004; Crews, 2002; Gasaway, 2001a; Huber, Yeh, and Jeweler, 2006; Lipinski, 2003). Ashley (2004) argued that at times a cost-benefit analysis may determine that compliance with the TEACH Act leads some educators to use simply the general fair use policies or seek copyright permission to avoid the hassles associated with the law. For instance, the law requires certain technological obligations from institutions such as finding ways to block students from keeping and distributing copyrighted materials. The problems arise when educators use copyrighted materials with high market value (for example, a popular movie or musical excerpt). In those instances, the odds of students' finding ways to circumvent the institution's system from reproduction and distribution become high. Rather than subjecting the institution to scrutiny, educators may opt to use more traditional ways of dealing with the fair use, pay for the license, or forgo the educational opportunity. Each case incurs pedagogical costs.

Kehoe (2005) asserted that the TEACH Act's limited application to nonprofit educational institutions fails to advance the goals of distance education because for-profit institutions are excluded from the TEACH Act. According to Kehoe, the exclusion of for-profit colleges is unnecessary. As he argued, the law's application to accredited institutions already ensures the legislator's purpose of meeting some educational standards. Moreover, the exclusion of for-profit colleges from the TEACH Act only stifles education, because according to Kehoe, for-profit schools are more inclined to try innovative teaching formats such as online education. Therefore, the law creates a barrier for the category of educational institutions that is most inclined to need fair use exceptions for online courses. The law's intentional exclusion of for-profit

EXHIBIT 1
Legal Parameters of the TEACH Act

Part I: Qualified Works and Amount of Fair Use

Does the copyrighted work fall under one of these categories? If so, the corresponding amount for fair use is listed below and proceed to Part II for further TEACH Act determination.

- Displays include an approach for multiple types of works including but not limited to pictorial, graphic, or sculptural works, images from a movie or slide, or an ebook. The amount of fair use for displays is the same as the fair use restrictions for a live classroom.
- Nondramatic literary or musical works - other than operas, music videos, and musicals - are not restricted for digital transmission of educational fair use materials. Nondramatic works include novels, poems, and music composition.
- Any other performances such as an opera, dance, play, or movie clips permit usage of reasonable and limited portions: "account for both the nature of the market for that type of work and the pedagogical purposes of the performance" (Senate Rep. 107-31, 2001 p. 8).

Qualified Work	displayed materials	nondramatic literary or musical work	any other performances
Amount of Usage	live classroom equivalent	not restricted	"reasonable and limited portions"

Part II: Instructional Conditions

Are the following instructional conditions met? If YES to the questions below, then proceed to Part III.

- Is the course under the direction or actual supervision of an instructor?
- Is the copyrighted work an integral part of class session?
- Does the class session serve as regular component to the systematic mediated instructional activities?
- Is the copyrighted work directly related and of material assistance to the teaching content?
- Are the instructional activities offered through an accredited, nonprofit educational institution?

(*Continued*)

EXHIBIT 1 (*Continued*)

Part III: Transmission Conditions: Access
Are the following transmission conditions met regarding access limits? If YES to the questions below, then proceed to Part IV.
- Is the transmission made sole purpose for students enrolled in the class?
- Is the transmission process limited as much as technically feasible?

Part IV: Transmission Conditions: Institutional Policies
Are the following transmission conditions met regarding access limits? If YES to the questions below, then proceed to Part V.
- Do the institution's copyright policies accurately describe the copyright laws?
- Do the institution's copyright policies promote compliance with copyright laws?
- Does the institution issue proper notice to students that materials used in course may have copyright protection?

Part V: Transmission Conditions: Institutional Policies
For digital transmissions, are the following copyright integrity measures taken? If YES to the questions below, then proceed to Part VI.
- Through technological measures, does the institution reasonably prevent retention beyond class session and unauthorized dissemination of works?
- Does the institution acknowledge that it does not participate in ways that would interfere with copyright owners' rights?

Part VI: Exceptions to the Exemption
Do the works used fall into one of the exceptions to the TEACH Act exemptions for fair use? If NO to the questions below, then the work and the conditions meet the TEACH Act.
- Is the work produced or marketed primarily for performance or display via digital networks and the institution knew or should have known of its illegality?
- Is the work a copy or phonorecord of performance or display not lawfully made or acquired and the institution knew or should have known of its illegality?

Source: Technology, Education, and Copyright Harmonization Act of 2002.

educational institutions, however, represents the interests of the book, music, and movie trade associations. That is, fair use permits limited use of copyrighted works with no royalties to the copyright holders. Accordingly, the TEACH Act simply indicates that, as a matter of national policy, copyright holders will forgo royalties in a set of limited circumstances when used by nonprofit, accredited educational institutions but that these copyright holders will not forgo these royalties as easily for for-profit educational institutions.

Finally, although the TEACH Act contains some imperfections, Crews (2002) articulated four ways in which the law improved past fair use provisions for distance education. Specifically, the TEACH Act expanded the scope of copyrightable subject matter that could fall under fair use; it extended the locations to more than just traditional classrooms; it did not bar students' retention of the works for a short period of time; and it permitted the conversion of analog works to digital format (Crews, 2002).

Implications About the Debate on Fair Use

With technological advances, accessibility to copyrighted works heightens the infringement activity in noninstructional contexts too, and these technologies also call for a reevaluation of institutional practices and the practicability of the copyright law. Sharing files, particularly of copyrighted music and movies, illustrates one problem in the growing debate about the law of fair use from the standpoint of how the intersection among three factors—existing legal parameters, technological advances, and differing viewpoints from various actors involved in the situation—shapes intellectual property policies and practices in higher education. Accordingly, this section discusses the uses of copyrighted material through sharing media files, the debates surrounding file sharing, and the associated challenges for colleges and universities.

Today, peer-to-peer software applications serve as one of the most frequent approaches to exchange of copyrighted products, and college and university networks have enabled these actions through their quick download speeds (Intellectual Property Institute, 2006; Kruger, 2004; Read, 2005a, 2005b; Student Monitor, 2007; Timiraos, 2006). As one court suggests, "approximately 90 percent of the content on [peer-to-peer] systems is copyrighted movies, software, images, and music disseminated without authorization" (*In re Charter Communications, Inc.* (2005), p. 773), and many of these activities occur on college campuses.

According to the Pew Internet and American Life Project, college students are more likely than the general population of Internet users to download music and share files. For example, in 2002, 14 percent of college students reported that they downloaded music, whereas only 4 percent of Internet users in 2001 generally engaged in such activity. Similarly, during those same years, 44 percent of college students reported that they share files online, compared with 26 percent of overall Internet users (Jones, 2002; see also Blue Coat Systems, 2004; Gross, 2005; Student Monitor, 2007; Timiraos, 2006). The amount of illegal file sharing among college students has therefore created legal problems for their institutions (Moore and McMullan, 2004; Read, 2006a, 2006b, 2007).

The trade associations and many copyright holders want the public to value copyrights, but attitudes about copyrights shape the adherence and respect for such rights. For instance, in 2000, the Pew Internet and American Life Project surveyed 6,413 Internet users and found that 64 percent of respondents between the ages of eighteen and twenty-nine believed downloading music for free was acceptable. Likewise, according to a 2003 study of randomly telephoned adults, a majority of students indicated that they were not inhibited by copyright restrictions when it comes to downloading and sharing files. Furthermore, in a comparison of full-time and part-time students, full-time students were more likely to indicate their lack of concern about copyright protections when downloading music.

According to a study from the Student Monitor (2007), 39 percent of full-time undergraduate students admitted to illegally downloading music or movies. Moreover, by some accounts, the location of choice is often the college campus (Intellectual Property Institute, 2006). According to the Intellectual Property Institute, college campuses ranked as the top location for illegal downloads of music through peer-to-peer applications. Data about the broadband method most frequently used for peer-to-peer music demonstrates a slightly different picture. Moore and McMullan (2004) report that students surveyed at one institution used dial-up modems and cable modems more often than the university network.

In light of the various data and news reports, universities are legitimately concerned, especially as copyright infringement can extend beyond the party who directly and actively engages in the wrongful act. Under federal law, liability exists for those who facilitate copyright infringement. Universities, as Internet service providers to their academic communities, potentially serve as facilitators to infringement activities through peer-to-peer networks. To deal with the research and teaching functions, the Digital Millennium Copyright Act includes a safe harbor provision for nonprofit higher education institutions that are service providers. The act states in relevant part:

(e) Limitation on liability of nonprofit educational institutions.— (1) When a public or other nonprofit institution of higher education is a service provider, and when a faculty member or graduate student who is an employee of such institution is performing a teaching or research function, for the purposes of subsections (a) and (b) such faculty member or graduate student shall be considered to be a person other than the institution, and for the purposes of subsections (c) and (d) such faculty member's or graduate student's knowledge or awareness of his or her infringing activities shall not be attributed to the institution, if:

(A) such faculty member's or graduate student's infringing activities do not involve the provision of online access to instructional materials that are or were required or recommended, within the preceding [three]-year period, for a course taught at the institution by such faculty member or graduate student;

(B) the institution has not, within the preceding [three]-year period, received more than two notifications described in subsection (c)(3) of claimed infringement by such faculty member or graduate student, and such notifications of claimed infringement were not actionable under subsection (f); and

(C) the institution provides to all users of its system or network informational materials that accurately describe, and promote compliance with, the laws of the United States relating to copyright [Digital Millennium Copyright Act, 17 U.S.C. §512(e) (2008)].

In other words, copyrighted materials retrieved through the network for teaching and research do not hold the institutional liable if the infringement did not take place in the preceding three years, the institution did not ignore three or more notices of past infringement from the same person, and the institution takes steps to comply with the copyright laws. Although the law shields educational service providers that comply with the outlined steps, copyright holders or their agents are contacting institutions of higher education through legal channels established under provisions of the Digital Millennium Copyright Act (DMCA).

Under the DMCA, copyright holders or their agents may serve a subpoena to an Internet service provider to identify the alleged infringer (17 U.S.C. §512(h) (2008)). Under that provision, the copyright holders along with their agents, particularly the trade associations for the recording, movie, software, gaming, photography, and image industries, have engaged in protecting copyright holders' interests in copyrighted works.[6] In particular, these organizations have sought action against college students and served universities as Internet service providers.

Two organizations in particular appear to be leading the charge to stop college students from illegal downloading through peer-to-peer applications: the Recording Industry Association of America (RIAA) and the Motion Picture Association of America (MPAA) (see, for example, Read, 2005a, 2005b). These organizations present two primary interests. First, they advocate the continuing existence of legal protection as a remedy to resolve copyright infringement disputes. Second, and more important, as Cary Sherman of the RIAA contends, they request fair compensation for the use of copyright holders' works.

These umbrella organizations support the continued protection and enforcement of intellectual property laws (Spanier and Sherman, 2005). Although some groups and individuals take the position that technology is changing and intellectual property rights should be reenvisioned (Electronic Frontier Foundation, 2007), copyright holders and their agents still argue that users of peer-to-peer applications, particularly college students who represent a significant population of this group, should respect the law and that the existing copyright law should govern the treatment of copyrighted works such as music, movies, images, and games. Furthermore, nonadherence to the copyright law often results in wrongfully appropriating works, and copyright infringements should be enforced through the law and campus policies as if they were thefts. Consequently, as a foundational strategy, the trade associations as agents and actual copyright holders went after the peer-to-peer software application companies.

In several landmark court cases against Napster and Grokster, the movie and music industry representatives went after the peer-to-peer providers (see *A&M Records, Inc.* v. *Napster, Inc.* (2000); *A&M Records, Inc.* v. *Napster, Inc.* (2001); and *M.G.M.* v. *Grokster* (2005)); today, copyright holders and their agents have targeted college students who have coordinated file-sharing devices. In 2003, the recording industry went after four college students at three different universities (Ahrens, 2003; Harmon, 2003). According to the RIAA, the college students directly participated in illegal downloading of copyrighted materials, and they operated a peer-to-peer system with music indexing features. Most important to college administrators, these events occurred on the university networks. Similarly, college students have increasingly participated in exchanges that try to evade the trade association spyware mechanisms by sharing files in college local area networks (Carlson, 2002; Read, 2006a).

Industry groups and copyright holders assert that they are losing sales because consumers are obtaining unlicensed materials, in particular through peer-to-peer file sharing (Kruger, 2004; Siwek, 2007). For instance, based on a convenience sample of 412 college students at four different urban universities, Rob and Waldfogel (2006) concluded that free music downloading sources result in at least a 10 percent loss of CD sales. The research demonstrates CD sales displacement, but the actual effects have come into question (see, for example, Madden and Lenhart, 2003; Oberholzer-Gee and Strumpf, 2007). Furthermore, several reports and empirical studies note the adverse financial impacts of piracy on the economy and corporate sales more broadly than just with CD sales. For instance, one estimate reports that in the music industry alone approximately 4 billion unlicensed downloads occurred in the United States in 2005 (Siwek, 2007).[7] When adjusted to account for estimated actual purchases and the retail margin calculations for lost sales, the report estimates losses from illegal music downloads to U.S. retailers of approximately $890 million. In addition, according to a state-by-state software privacy study, the report indicated that "piracy cost more than 105,000 jobs, or $5.3 billion in lost wages, during 2002" (Kruger, 2004, p. 48). Of course, the various methods of piracy are not considered in this calculation, yet reproduction on a CD likely accounts for a significant portion of the impact. Furthermore, these groups are abundantly clear that piracy plays a huge role in hurting the employment conditions and wages of actors, directors, publicists, distributors, artists, composers, producers, software designers, and retailers, including small, independent college-town music stores (see, for example, Carlson, 2003). Put simply, it is often argued that the loss of sales revenue affects industry employment patterns, corporate performance through loss earnings, and reduced tax revenues (Siwek, 2007).

Although use of the DMCA raises questions about particular organizations' business practices (Carlson, 2003; Chmielewski, 2003), some preliminary data indicate desirable outcomes for the entertainment industry (Madden and Lenhart, 2003). For example, according to Madden and Rainie (2005), recording industry lawsuits and letters of potential lawsuits against peer-to-peer users have reduced copyright piracy. In particular, the report indicates a drop in use of peer-to-peer file sharing, such as Grokster, Kazaa, WinMX, and BearShare. More important, the authors state that music downloading among students and other groups has dropped sharply. The authors suggest two reasons to account for the declines in peer-to-peer file sharing. First, the chart tracked when RIAA lawsuit threats started and of actual lawsuits initiated against peer-to-peer users, and it noted declines in peer-to-peer piracy following those legal actions. Second, the increasing availability and subscription to fee-based online music services have provided an outlet for proper license venues.

Several reports and articles indicate movements in higher education to respond to these infringements, including education about copyright, enforcement of laws, alternative means to piracy, and digital network management (see, for example, "Reducing Peer-to-Peer (P2P) Piracy on University Campuses," 2005; "Piracy on University Networks," 2007). First, educational seminars, student service programs, and notices about copyright infringement address issues surrounding perceptions about downloading and file swapping as well as understanding the laws and policies of copyright (Kruger, 2004; Lane and Hendrickson, 2005; Lane and Healy, 2005; Lenhart and Fox, 2000; Moore and McMullan, 2004; O'Donnell and Parker, 2005; Read, 2007).

Second, colleges and universities have issued "take-down" notices (that is, warning notices that an illegal activity is likely occurring so the infringer must cease and "take down" the infringing network mechanism), pursuant to DMCA when infringement activities occur over their networks ("Reducing Peer-to-Peer (P2P) Piracy on University Campuses," 2005; "Piracy on University Networks," 2007). Third, numerous institutions implemented legal music downloading services for their community to use (Spanier and Sherman, 2005; Read, 2007). The primary intent of this approach is to support students through legal means and avoid the piracy entanglement between the entertainment industry and students (Read, 2007). Although these services do not completely eliminate media piracy (Timiraos, 2006), they still provide a legal avenue for music available on those networks ("Reducing Peer-to-Peer (P2P) Piracy on University Campuses," 2005; "Piracy on University Networks," 2007). Fourth, colleges and universities have adopted practices that moderate or curb file swapping (Liebowitz, 2002). For example, one approach includes managing bandwidth use during traditionally heavy periods of downloading and during critical times for university operations. In addition, more sophisticated software monitors file swapping or unusually heavy bandwidth use, typically associated with downloading media. Finally, pursuant to the Higher Education Act, colleges and universities continue their measures to combat illegal downloading of copyrighted materials, including using technology-based deterrents and offering legal alternatives to accessing music, movies, and other protected downloaded works.

The peer-to-peer file-sharing problem represents more than simply illegal downloading of music and movies. First, the situation signals a major shift in attitudes about copyrightable works. Many college students and others acknowledge their actions and defend those actions. Some even question whether easy access to materials qualifies as fair use through a pseudo-public domain. Second, parties with an interest in the copyrighted works do not hesitate to involve colleges and universities in their pursuits. Third, the severity of the problem requires federal legislation to mandate controls in universities to curb the activities. Fourth, as technology advances, this problem is likely to filter into other disputes that may involve colleges and universities with video game owners, publishers of e-books, and even copyright holders who work for the institution. Fifth, this situation clearly depicts our framework of how technological capacities, actor-based interests, and existing legal parameters shape college and university intellectual property policies and practices.

Chapter Summary

This chapter presented the challenges for colleges and universities when technology, law, and competing interests intersect. Technological advancements alter the way the higher education community works; the law sets the parameters in what constitutes fair use; and multiple interests arise over the uses of copyrighted materials and their access. In this instance, the difficulty is illustrated with a fundamental question: How does a university serve as educator and industry monitor? The technological changes altered the economic, political, and social environment for the higher education community. Consequently, while addressing the fair use and nonfair use of copyrighted works in instructional and noninstructional contexts, this chapter drew attention to the problems faced in higher education over copyrighted works.

This chapter illustrated the lack of legal clarity in fair use; the role of lawsuits to alter behavior by the current subpoenas issued to students for peer-to-peer file swapping; the contested terrain of various copyrighted works, especially as evidenced from the CONFU guidelines that could not reach consensus and the distinctions between the treatments of sound recordings and musical works; the mandated practices (for example, guidelines), processes (for example, TEACH Act provisions), and materials (for example, software) to monitor potential copyright infringement and interfere when it occurs; and the significance of commercial value such as sales displacement from peer-to-peer file swapping and course packs as substitutes to anthologies over the noncommercial values associated with moral rights (that is, attribution and integrity).

Finally, the copyright discussion comes with a caveat. This chapter did not capture the relationship between technological advancements and their corresponding effects on college and university libraries. Although the chapter mentioned some impact on library services, much more could be said but is beyond the scope of this monograph. Those impacts are numerous, perhaps warranting their own monograph.

The Law of Patents

THE PATENT HOLDER possesses the exclusive rights to use, sell, produce, and distribute the patented subject matter. With such levels of control over the invention as well as the corresponding rewards attached to the invention such as royalties, actors who participate in the creation or discovery phases often desire some interest in it. In addition, as technology changes, the role and coverage of patents become refined as policies and practices in academic communities also change. Accordingly, this chapter articulates the legal elements of patent law, highlights the evolving judicial and federal agency interpretations of patent law in light of technological shifts, explains the impact of university patents on academic communities and other key actors, and describes some important legislative and institutional policy proposals.

Patent Law

Unlike a copyright, which exists immediately upon the fixing of an expression in a tangible medium, a patent is a document issued by the U.S. Patent and Trademark Office that grants a monopoly on use to the owner of the patent. To understand patent law, this section surveys key elements of patent law by discussing the legal conditions to qualify for a patent and rights available to patent holders.

Types of Patents

The federal law recognizes three types of patents: utility, design, and plant. Each statutory category for patents establishes qualifications and requirements as well as the length of time for the protection. The most frequently applied patent is the utility patent. A utility patent applies to an invention or discovery that is a new and useful machinery, manufactured article, composition of matter, process, or new and useful improvement of a process or product. Sample filings of utility patents from higher education institutions include the University of Minnesota's creation of the seat belt, Stanford and the University of California's joint project on recombinant DNA, Columbia University's discovery of a process for inserting DNA into eukaryotic cells and producing proteinaceous material, Georgetown's creation of the CT scan, and Clark University's creation of rocket fuel. The protection period for a utility patent is twenty years.

A design patent protects original creations of an ornamental design applied to a manufactured article such as a chair configuration, handheld phone, or computer. Its period of protection is only fourteen years. And a plant patent provides protection for inventions and discoveries of new and distinct varieties of plants, which may reproduce asexually. In higher education, these filings include the University of California's avocado cultivars, Pennsylvania State University's mushroom plants, and Cornell University's specialized raspberry plants. A plant patent lasts for twenty years. Although each statutory category for patents establishes qualifications and requirements, a patentable product or process may qualify for more than one statutory category. In those instances, the patent filer must clearly specify each reference component to describe its form and function for the respective patent type.

Patentable Subject Matter

To qualify for a patent, the product or process must conform to two general classes of requirements in terms of form and qualities. First, the patentable subject matter must be in the form of a machine, manufactured article, composition of matter, or process (35 U.S.C. §101 (2008)).

Machinery. The law refers to machinery as equipment or mechanical devices that maintain multiple components to construct or create an end product. Thus, when scientists at the University of Texas at Austin improved the homopolar generator, a machine that generates the same levels of polarity from magnetic forces, the university filed for a patent for it.

Manufactured articles. Manufactured articles represent humanly constructed products, including items created through machinery or some other type of nonnatural process. The end product must be some physical manifestation such as an ergonomic chair. With scientific advancements, items that constitute manufactured articles are expanding. For instance, in *Diamond* v. *Chakrabarty* (1980), the U.S. Supreme Court held that the creation of a new bacterium qualified as a patentable manufactured article. Although the substance dealt with living organisms, which are not patentable under the law, the Court rationalized that the bacteria result from genetic engineering and derive from a scientific laboratory. This case expands dramatically the categories of patentable matter.

Compositions of matter. This category involves the mixture of chemicals or other substances in an effort to transform the elements into a new matter. For example, chemical mixtures of prescription drugs, drinks, and lotions are all patentable.

Processes. A process is also patentable. A process involves steps, methods, and even artful construction of activities that may result in tangible items. According to *State Street Bank and Trust Co.* v. *Signature Financial Group* (1998), a sophisticated business method constitutes a patentable subject matter. In this case, a computer program that structured investment packages sufficiently met the requirements for a patentable process. Similarly, computer software that produces useful, tangible outputs has also been awarded patent protections under the category of patentable processes.

Second, in addition to the form that the invention must take, under the law the invention must meet the three quality criteria of novelty, nonobviousness, and utility. The criterion for novelty requires (1) that the invention not already exist or be previously described, (2) that it be reduced to practice to display the invention's functionality, and (3) that it be filed with the U.S. Patent and Trademark Office within one year of its revelation. Accordingly, under the statutory provisions covered under the criterion for novelty, the patent examiner typically asks the following questions: Was the invention invented or described earlier? Is the invention reduced into practice to display the invention's functionality? Did the inventor file within one year from revealing the invention?

Under the condition for novelty, the federal patent law establishes a priority rule to determine the status of the patent holder (35 U.S.C. §102 (2008)). In the United States, the priority rule for the novelty criterion defaults to the party that created or discovered the product or process first. Although many advanced nation-states such as Canada, France, Germany, and Japan operate under a first to file priority rule, the United States adopts a first to *invent* priority rule (Ubel, 1994). That is, the inventor who first creates or discovers the patentable subject receives the rights.

The debate over the first to invent versus the first to file priority rule dates back to early statutory proposals (see, for example, Frost, 1967). Today, Congress continues to entertain revisions to the policy of first to invent with discussions of aligning this nation's patent policies with those of other industrialized nations, that is, a first-to-file priority rule. Although this policy shift is not likely to occur, if it does, universities may increase their patent support staff in technology transfer offices to address the timing issue, particularly because higher education institutions would be competing for time against industry, which has more available staff per scientist.

Putting aside the debate, under current U.S. patent law the priority rule for patent filings relies on a principle of "first to invent." Consequently, before issuance of a patent, the patent officer determines whether an earlier filing or some other prior knowledge of the patent subject exists. In legal jargon, the patent officer inquires into the "prior art" or the "state of the art." As knowledge about prior art may not be identical in description or contain precise details, the patent officer examines the components and description of the patentable subject for comparison with other filings to determine whether "prior art references" are mentioned because of close links or whether the patent filing is not novel because prior art exists.

References to prior art may occur in journal articles, conference presentations, dissertations, grant applications, or media reports (Garabedian, 2002). Furthermore, they are not limited to documents available in the United States or in existing patent filings. In fact, *In re Hall* (1986) involved the denial of a patent to an enzyme because a prior publication described the enzyme. The publication, a doctoral dissertation, was available at Freiburg University in Germany. The U.S. scientist declared no knowledge of the study, and evidence submitted demonstrated that the dissertation was available only as a "single catalogued thesis in one university library," which made its accessibility very limited (p. 898). Nevertheless, the patent filer could have had access to the prior publication, and a prior publication disqualifies a patent issuance. Thus, the application was denied.

Besides being the first to create or discover an invention, the federal patent law requires the inventor to put the invention into practice. A written description of the patentable subject matter satisfies the practice requirement of the law. Basically, the policy mandates that information appear sufficient so that one may test the functionality of the product or process and that the description appear with adequate references to determine whether another product or process is related or identical to the patent being sought.

In addition, the patent filing must occur within one year of initially revealing the invention. As a matter of policy, the one-year grace period provides sufficient time for the inventor to file the patent, and it also places sufficient limits so inventors cannot delay filing as a strategy to extend the patent protection period. Furthermore, the law precludes the patenting of products and processes in public use or on sale more than a year from the initial invention (35 U.S.C. §102(b) (2008)).

A second criterion for quality for patentable subject matter involves nonobviousness. To evaluate the subject matter's obviousness, the review consists of three interactive components. According to *Graham v. John Deere Co. of Kansas City* (1966), the nonobvious criterion relies on the relationship among prior art, the patent subject matter, and experts who possess ordinary skill in a field or craft. Another way to view the nonobviousness criterion is to ask to what extent prior art informed others of the pending patent's subject matter? Does the invention reveal something more than what has already been established? Did the typical person in a craft or field already possess the skills to invent the subject matter?

A third quality criterion for patentable subject matter requires the invention to be useful. The usefulness criterion requires the utility with a readily apparent purpose. According to the eighth edition of *Manual of Patent*

Examining Procedure (U.S. Patent and Trademark Office, 2007), the purpose may be explicit or implicit. Despite those guidelines, the courts and the U.S. Patent and Trademark Office consistently articulate utility in the form of a specific and substantial nature. The specific utility component requires "a well-defined and particular benefit to the public" (*In re Fisher*, 2005, p. 1371). Besides the criteria of novelty, nonobviousness, and usefulness, the courts have articulated that nonpatentable subject matter includes abstract ideas, laws of nature, mathematical equations without applications, and natural phenomena (*Gottschalk v. Benson* (1972)).

Patent Filing

Besides the requirements for the patentable subject matter form and qualities, the patent filing requires documentation of "specification" and "claims" (35 U.S.C. §112 (2008)). Specification refers to adequacy in the patent description so that others in the craft may replicate the invention. Furthermore, the patent instrument must contain the stated claims of the invention or what the invention accomplishes. To do so, the written description must include the various structural or physical characteristics and their properties, and it must spell out the elements of the invented product or process and its functionality.

In practice, the specification and claims components of a patent application mandate a detailed instrument, particularly for a biotechnology patent application. In *Regents of the University of California* v. *Eli Lilly and Co.* (1997), the issue related to whether the university had "possession" of the invention. The rationale for this standard is to prevent a patent holder from later extending the capacity of the patent with assertions that its patent covers some process or product not explicitly indicated on the initial patent application (Holman, 2007). With that policy in mind, the judges in *Regents of the University of California* v. *Eli Lilly and Co.* crafted an interpretation of the written description requirement in which transference of information from one context to another was not acceptable. The researchers used recombinant DNA technology to extract rat insulin, and based on the researchers' belief that the process concept would be transferable to humans, they also filed a patent with the same procedures to extract human insulin. According to the court, the patent application contained sufficient description for the rat insulin treatment process but lacked the required description for the human insulin patent. It noted that the description required a "precise definition, such as by structure, formula, or chemical name, of claimed subject matter sufficient to distinguish it from other materials" (p. 1566), and in this instance the description indicated only a general method to extract a synthesized DNA sample, known as cDNA, encoding human insulin. Although the description contained sufficient information about the process, the court indicated that more information regarding the properties and characteristics of the microorganism connected with the process was needed in the patent. In this case, which is still good law, the court declared that a very detailed written description of related scientific properties and characteristics must be indicated in the patent application. For many, this written description standard raises the bar for patents, especially for biotechnology patents, as the articulation of structural sequences of particular genes from a patented process is extremely difficult (Holman, 2007). Nevertheless, the trend in court decisions appears to move toward greater and more specific details.

In many past cases, the details in the written description also permitted some inference or imputation of information to individuals who are skilled in the craft (see, for example, Merges and Nelson, 1990, 1994). As such, the written description did not have to recite every piece of information, provided an enabling disclosure standard was met (that is, the application contained clear enough details for an individual with ordinary skills of the trade to replicate or use the invention). In *University of Rochester* v. *G. D. Searle* (2004), Rochester claimed that Searle and several other pharmaceutical companies infringed on its patent. The patent covered a treatment method selectively using Cox-2 inhibitors to reduce inflammation while also reducing side effects such as stomach ulcers, bleeding, and irritation that existed with other treatments. The pharmaceutical companies successfully argued that no infringement occurred because Rochester's patent was invalid. They claimed that the patent description did not disclose the compounds needed to achieve the intended outcome, and they contended that Rochester was stretching its patent coverage. In response, Rochester asserted that it did sufficiently describe the method and that scientists with ordinary skills in the field could properly administer the methods and achieve the same results. The court disagreed with

Rochester. It concluded that Rochester's method depended on a specific compound, which was not articulated in the patent. Consequently, the court invalidated the patent. Thus, this case indicates that generalizations in a patent without specific claims cannot be upheld; otherwise, those patent holders could assert a patent's purpose that was not intended or recognized at the time of the patent filing.

Patent Ownership and Rights

By default, federal patent laws presumptively assume that the first inventor files and receives the patent. This filing pursuant to federal patent law determines the proper inventor, but it does not always identify the owner of the invention or the rightful holder of the patent. Because a patent is a property right, state law governs—as it generally does in dealing with all property rights (Kaplin and Lee, 2006). Typically, in cases dealing with property interests, particularly for patents, those interests are determined through the applicable state's contract law.

Indeed, inventors may enter into a contract to assign (that is, transfer) their rights to another party, which usually occurs between inventors and their employer.[8] At many universities, the inventor is required to disclose both the invention and to assign (that is, transfer) his or her rights to the university (Korn, 1987). For example, a university intellectual property policy may explicitly state that inventions created with any university resources belong to the university. Likewise, a university employment agreement may explicitly state that employees, including academic researchers, are hired for the express purpose of creating, discovering, and inventing products and processes for commercial and intellectual purposes. Such statements through an employment contract present expectations of ownership rights to employees' inventions. In short, the law of contracts dictates the ownership rights.

Contract law is primarily interpreted through applicable state laws, not federal laws; thus, the determinations may vary somewhat from state to state. Nevertheless, some general contract law principles apply (Drechsler, 2008; Weidemier, 2007). For one, an express agreement represents the clearest form of ownership determination. A university employment contract between the employer and employee serves as an expressed agreement to articulate the intentions of the parties regarding ownership and corresponding rights to inventions. Second, express terms in a contract with an industry research sponsor often spell out the ownership rights, related distributions, and controls over the invention.

In rare instances, a state university's policies may be equivalent to a state statute. In *Kucharczyk* v. *Regents of the University of California* (1996), the court indicated that the University's status as a state constitutional agency makes its policies akin to state statutes. Despite this elevated category of university policies, the court's analysis followed state contract law interpretations.

When express terms for patent ownership are not given in the contract, implied terms or an implied contract might exist. According to Weidemier (2007), an implied agreement governing patent ownership usually occurs in one of three ways: (1) the individual was hired to invent, (2) the individual was hired to solve a specific problem, or (3) the individual served the employer in a fiduciary capacity. For example, in *Regents of the University of New Mexico* v. *Knight* (2003), the court ruled that the university and the academic scientists had an implied contract. Under New Mexico contract law, employment policies constitute an implied contract, and as evidence of an agreement the university cited language from the employment contracts, its patent policy, and coinventor agreements to demonstrate that inventors are required to assign patents to the university. The court concluded that the university owned the inventions in question. Similarly, even when no employment arrangement exists for others in the academic community, such as with graduate or undergraduate research assistants, the law generally interprets an implied contract based on the student handbook or other prevailing policy documents (but see Patel, 1996).

When no agreement can be located either through expressed or implied terms, a university may assert "shop rights" if the invention was made using the university's equipment, facilities, or other resources (Drechsler, 2008). "Shop rights" permit employers to use an invention created by its employees when the invention used resources from the "shop." By operation of law, a quasi-contract is recognized, and the employer receives a nonexclusive license through the shop right privilege. The focus is on employment conditions, not necessarily the status of the employee. Therefore, part-time staff and employed students such as graduate research assistants could meet the standard for colleges and universities to seek shop rights (see, for example, *University of West Virginia Board of Trustees* v. *Vanvoorhies,* 2002). In addition, under contract law universities may specify in their handbooks the required assignment of rights to all inventions created by the university community when campus resources are used.

Coinventor Status

An invention may involve more than one inventor, and the law in this case reflects the conflicts associated with patenting. Under the law, coinventors apply and declare inventor status jointly (35 U.S.C. §116 (2008)). The standard for qualifying for joint inventions is high, and one's mere participation in the inventive works alone is insufficient. In *Stern* v. *Trustees of Columbia University* (2006), the court drew from past cases to articulate the standards for joint inventorship and indicated that each joint inventor must generally contribute to the conception of the invention. In this case, Stern, a former medical student at Columbia University, assisted a professor for one semester with a research project that used prostaglandins to reduce intraocular pressure as a treatment for glaucoma. The professor later patented the glaucoma treatments and assigned the inventions to the university. Stern then learned of the patents and sued the professor and the university, claiming joint inventorship.

The legal presumption is that nonlisted inventors are not coinventors. Consequently, the burden was on the student to prove otherwise. The legal burden falls between the preponderance of evidence in most civil trials and beyond a reasonable doubt required of criminal cases. In this case, the former student attested to the experiments that he carried out, but the court determined that he was unaware of certain claims made on the patent application and held that Stern was not a joint inventor.

In prior rulings, joint inventor claims were dismissed when an individual who claims to be the inventor assigns patent ownership to another party such as a university (Patel, 1996; Seymore, 2006a, 2006b). In these cases, the university typically holds the patent rights, and the courts have held that the claimed coinventors have no standing to challenge the rights that were assigned to them. In *Chou* v. *University of Chicago* (2001), however, the court permitted a claimed coinventor's challenge over the assignment of rights because the coinventor indicated that although she would assign her rights to the university per the employment agreement, her inclusion as a named coinventor was critical to her reputation in the scientific community. Consequently, in this case the court held that the claimed coinventor, who was also a graduate student, could pursue her action to be named as a coinventor even though questions of ownership were not at issue. For many, this case also stood for the proposition that graduate students could not be taken advantage of by their faculty advisor (Patel, 1996; Seymore, 2006a, 2006b).

In biopharmaceutical inventions, the law is well established that coinventors must have "knowledge of both the specific chemical structure of the compound and an operative method of making it" (*Board of Education* v. *American Bioscience, Inc.*, 2003, pp. 1341–1342). In a case challenging inventorship status for the cancer treatment drug Taxol, several scientists who were at Florida State University as lab participants in the drug's development sued the university for inclusion as joint inventors. In that case, the court provided additional legal guidance in joint inventor claims. Specifically, it declared that "teaching skills or general methods that somehow facilitate a later invention, without more, does not render one a coinventor" (*Board of Education* v. *American Bioscience, Inc.*, 2003, pp. 1341–1342).

In light of the patent joint inventor qualifications, differences between the list of authors who write about academic inventions in a publication and the list of coinventors declared on patent applications can be expected. Normative behaviors in the academic-scientific field often list numerous authors on articles in which one or more authors played a relatively minor role in the publication. Although that standard suffices for the academic-scientific publishing arena, it is insufficient to qualify as a coinventor of a patent. As discussed, the patent filing requires the claimed coinventors to show that they actively participated in the invention's conception, formulation, and understanding.

The Research Exemption

Patent law exempts certain acts from infringement claims. Under the experimental use exemption, researchers may use patented inventions in very limited circumstances. According to the law, under the experimental use exemption a party without any legal approval from the patent holder or its assignee may still use a patented invention provided that its use is "solely for amusement, to satisfy idle curiosity, or for strictly philosophical inquiry" (*Madey v. Duke University,* 2002, p. 1362). One might argue that university research and instruction would fall into the experimental use exemption, yet in 2002 the court in *Madey* ruled that the experimental use exemption did not apply to Duke University. According to the court, the research exemption to patent infringement does not apply when use of the patented product is in further-ance of a university's business activities. Because the projects that required the use of the patented product furthered the "institution's legitimate business objectives, including educating and enlightening students and faculty partic-ipating in these projects," the court did not accept Duke's argument that its activities fell into the research exemption (*Madey,* 2002, p. 1362). Thus, the use of the invention amounted to a patent infringement.

The case centered around two patents. Before working at Duke Univer-sity, Madey invented two free electron laser technologies while at Stanford University and retained full patent rights to those inventions. When Madey arrived at Duke, he directed the free electron laser research lab and used equip-ment under his patent ownership. After a decade as director of the lab and a bitter dispute, Duke officials removed Madey as the lab director. As a result, Madey resigned, but Duke continued to use the two patented free electron laser technologies, which led to the lawsuit.

Duke's primary argument rested on the acceptable use of patents for "research, academic, or experimental purposes" (*Madey,* 2002, p. 1361). As further support of the exemption to patent infringements, the university argued that its nonprofit status plays a role. The appellate court disagreed. The court emphasized the narrow application of the experimental use exemp-tion to instances of general inquiry without any business engagement. The court interpreted the academic research laboratory's activities with the patented technologies as furthering the legitimate business activities of the university (Eisenberg, 2003). Thus, the experimental use exemption did not apply, and the court ruling determined that Duke's actions amounted to patent infringement.

Besides contributing to the patent thicket problem (see the next chapter for a discussion of patent thickets), academic researchers who conducted basic research often bypassed intellectual property rights and ignored the patent thicket problem because they asserted a research exemption (Yancey and Stewart, 2007). That is, they simply used patented products and processes because they assumed a research exemption protected them. In 2002, the U.S. Court of Appeals for the Federal Circuit declared that the research exemption does not exist as broadly as researchers had thought.

Madey illustrates how commercialization of research undermines the very activity needed to commercialize the research: research itself. In other words, the research exemption in patent law allows for a kind of "fair use" of patented inventions. But if the institution promotes such use for the purposes of seeking commercial gain, then the research exemption may be nullified and may actually subject itself to a patent infringement lawsuit. Such activities highlight the conflicts associated with patenting specifically and intellectual property generally. Moreover, engaging in research activities to educate students, further faculty interests, "increase the status of the institution[,] and lure lucrative research grants" as well as top quality students and faculty, thereby disqualifies academic institutions from asserting the research or experimental use exemption over patented products and processes (*Madey*, 2002, p. 1362). Put simply, the laws are narrowing circumstances that qualify using patented products and processes under the research exemption, and the courts increasingly recognize the commercial nature of higher education for private interests.

Copyrights and Patents: Computer Software

In certain cases, the invention, which is also placed on a fixed medium, falls under both copyright and patent protections. The legal questions associated with these cases are even more complex because individuals are uncertain about which laws and guidelines apply. Innovations in technology thus constrain the application of existing laws and in turn present more contentious and uncertain situations in higher education. One particular technology highlights this problem: computer software.

Computer software is expensive to develop but easy to copy, making it vulnerable to piracy (Bhattacharjee, Gopal, and Sanders, 2003; Gross, 2005; Schacht, 2006). The United States was the first nation to actively protect software; however, extensive debates occurred about whether software should be protected under copyright or patent law or some other law. Proponents of copyright law argue that computer software is simply another form of "writing" brought about by technological changes. Proponents of patent protection argue that the effort and functional uses of software are more analogous to inventive activity than to artistic creation. Others argue that neither copyrights nor patents are analogous in such a case and that some special kind of protection is necessary. In the United States, the decision came down primarily in favor of copyright protection, and in 1980 the Copyright Act of 1976 was amended to explicitly cover software (Wallerstein, Mogee, and Schoen, 1993).[9] The debate lingered on as to whether software qualified for a patent. After decades of debates and mixed court messages on whether software constituted a patentable subject matter, the U.S. Supreme Court ruled in *Diamond* v. *Diehr* (1981) that a computer program used to recalibrate a production method qualified for a patent. Consequently, computer software would be protected with a patent and a copyright.

During the early development of computer software programs, the higher education community infrequently raised concerns over issues about proprietary rights. To the extent that there were proprietary rights, they tended to be enforced by restrictive trade secret licensing agreements (Samuelson, 1993). Four significant developments in the 1980s, however, changed the landscape of the software industry and intellectual property rights. First, the growth of personal computers led to the increasing need for software. Second, the commercial success of early software for personal computers such as Visicalc and Lotus 1–2–3 also increased activity in this area. Third, the legal decision to offer protection of software under copyright law and the decision of the Copyright Office to discontinue its policy of requiring that the full text of source codes be deposited with it permitted the full disclosure of the software without the need to resort to trade secrecy. Finally, the decision of the Patent and Trademark Office to start issuing patents to software gave added protection to software and led to the proliferation of patents (Samuelson, 1993).

Computer programs are controversial because the type of protection they warrant is under debate. Because they can be easily reproduced and copied, copyright protection makes sense, but it raises questions because, say, decompilation (common with patented information for design improvement) would be problematic as reproduction itself would constitute infringement. Some patents have been granted for software, but perhaps only if it is adequately embodied in a machine (such as the iPhone) or adequately restricted to a particular range of applications (Barton, 1993).

Institutional Patent Policies

To determine the rightful owner of patentable works created at colleges and universities, parties may not find helpful answers from the law of copyright or patents. Instead, laws pertaining to contract law may be more instructive, and institutional patent policies serve as one source to figure out the terms of the contractual arrangement if an explicit agreement does not exist.

As institutions of higher education recognized the value of patent protection for academic research, university patent policies emerged on campuses across the nation. This development was noticeable. In 1934, Palmer published one of the early studies of university patent policies and practices at more than twenty U.S. universities and the University of Toronto. He found that most universities in his sample did not have a patent policy in place and that patent determinations were made case by case. But by the latter part of the 1950s, eighty-five universities had some form of patent policy in place. Much of the movement occurred because the National Research Council encouraged and even advocated for patent policies so that inventions would be protected and controlled by the academic community (Robbins, 2006). In addition, a provision in the Bayh-Dole Act of 1980 requires nonprofit universities that file for patents to maintain policies regarding rights and responsibilities over the inventions. Today it is highly unlikely that any institution does not maintain patent policies, even if it engages in a low level of research activity (Korn, 1987).

With the increasing adoption of university patent policies, several papers have examined the content of entire institutional patent policies (see, e.g.,

Audette, 1980; Bowers and Leon, 1994; Heathington, Heathington, and Roberson, 1986; National Association of College and University Business Officers, 1978; Sun, 2008). For instance, in 1978, the National Association of College and University Business Officers published a report of intellectual property policies at thirteen research universities (Boston University, California Institute of Technology, Cornell University, Massachusetts Institute of Technology, Purdue University, Rockefeller University, University of California, University of Connecticut, University of Georgia, University of Pennsylvania, University of Southern California, University of Virginia, and Washington University). The report briefly commented on selected aspects of the policies and attached copies of the policies. Taking those 1978 policies, Sun (2008) analyzed and compared them with the 2008 policies of the same thirteen research universities. Sun found significant similarities in the framing of these policies' purposes and the legal provisions governing the patent rights. For example, the policies from 1978 and 2008 justified their patenting purposes around three principal concerns: patenting for the public good, supporting scientific talent, and addressing the needs of economic development (see also Bowers and Leon, 1994; Metlay, 2006; Rhoades and Slaughter, 1991). In addition, nearly all of these policies in 1978 and in 2008 included provisions regarding invention disclosure requirements, the role of the technology transfer office, ownership rights, and distribution over licensing royalties and equity. Some differences existed, though most appeared negligible. For instance, with regard to the urgency of invention disclosures, only two of the patent policies in place by 1978 expressed urgency and expressly mandated disclosures. By 2008, all thirteen institutions conveyed clear requirements to disclose and language that indicated expediency in the disclosure process. Similarly, the 1978 and 2008 policies discussed royalties, but in the 2008 policies, a few institutions changed their basis for calculation from gross to net amounts.

With a larger sample, Bowers and Leon (1994) examined sixty-five institutional policies from primarily high-activity research universities. Their analysis illustrated the diversity in policy language while also highlighting the primary provisions contained in these policies, particularly sections that addressed equity rights of universities, procedures for distribution of patent policies and disclosure of inventions, and income distribution to inventors. The study highlighted particular characteristics and approaches to framing patent policies. First, the policies contained generalized themes, particularly about the universities' interest in inventions. For instance, sixty-two of the sixty-five policies expressed institutional rights to the inventions of faculty, staff, or students. In addition, these institutions specified an interest when inventors use significant university resources. Furthermore, many of the institutions expect their faculty and staff to disclose inventions. Because these provisions appear with high frequency among the policies, they signal some standardization among policies. Second, although many of the policies differ in how they structure and share revenue derived from the intellectual property, this article revealed several ways to structure distribution of revenues at least as the policy committees set the arrangements back in 1993. Third, Bowers and Leon acknowledged that in several instances the policy audience and policy purposes differed. For instance, according to the authors, Louisiana State University's policy addressed rights of external sponsors, while many of the other policies conveyed institutional priority over faculty, staff, or student rights. Fourth, Bowers and Leon highlighted special provisions contained in the policies, which also identified interested parties and institutional priorities. For instance, at the University of Mississippi, the policy requires the university to favor state firms when engaging in technology transfer, which is likely consistent with the state's other government contract priorities and is aligned with its role as an economic engine in the state.

The challenge in studying patent policies, very broadly, is that generalizations are very difficult to draw (see, for example, Fine and Castagnera, 2003). Bowers and Leon (1994) and Sun (2008) examined numerous patent policies in their entirety, and they all concluded that many of the policies contained similar overarching headings but that variations in key provisions existed in areas such as royalty distribution and interested parties. Each institution structures its policies to meet particular interests (for example, intellectual property committees or individual administrators who crafted the language to meet certain institutional concerns) or to adhere to the specifics of its state's laws.

Rather than examining the entire institutional patent policies to locate broad overarching similarities, several articles examine a particular concept captured in the policies. These studies attempted to establish categories in a given concept to capture the various ways to determine ownership. Under one approach, the researcher analyzed institutional patent policies from a resource frame (Chew, 1992). Based on the resources used, ownership of patentable works followed. For that study, Chew (1992) surveyed the patent policies of twenty universities with the largest research expenditures during the 1987 fiscal year plus seven other research universities that fall under the Carnegie Classification of doctoral institutions. Chew observed three categories of intellectual property policies designed to differentiate patent ownership. In one set of policies, which she referred to as resource-providers, institutions based their claims to ownership on the amount of university resources used. Typically, if the inventor used significant university resources, the invention would become university property. In another set of policies, known as maximalists, universities asserted ownership rights when one of two conditions were met: either university resources were used or inventing was part of the creator's employment. The final group of intellectual property policies justified extensive university ownership. Known as the supramaximalists, these institutional policies took ownership of all faculty work created during employment, whether or not the invention was created during faculty personal time. Chew pointed out that often universities permitted faculty to have, use, or keep a portion of the royalties but a general presumption existed that "the university, as the employer, owns faculty research" (p. 261).

In another approach, the researcher analyzed institutional patent policies based on employment arrangements. Using this frame, Smith (1997) argued that the determination of ownership begins with an examination of any state statutes that might apply or language from a contractual agreement that addresses assignment of inventions to employers. Without it, he explained that claims to ownership derive from common law (that is, case law). According to Smith, the case law identifies three types of employment arrangements associated with different intellectual property ownership or rights to the intellectual property. In one employment arrangement, when an employee is explicitly hired to invent, the employee's inventions belong to the university. Smith referred to this employment arrangement as "specific inventive employment." In another employment arrangement, an employee would have responsibilities to carry out "research," "design," or "development." For this arrangement, the inventor would retain ownership rights, but the employer would obtain shop rights or a nonexclusive privilege to use the invention. Smith labeled this employment arrangement "general inventive employment." In a third category, the employment arrangement is such that the employee works without any expectation to invent. In such instances, known as "general employment," the inventor retains the rights and the university has no legal rights to the invention. Of course, all these rules about patent ownership beg the question of the power struggles associated with patenting, which are important for determining the nature of the agreements established in institutions.

Questions of Ownership: Faculty Versus Administrators

The construction of intellectual property policies illustrates the competing interests and the impending power struggles among the parties to university-based inventions (see, for example, Mendoza and Berger, 2005; Rhoades and Slaughter, 1991). At one level, the power struggles highlight the authority structures, particularly under the law. Because employment and contract laws dictate the ownership and corresponding rights (for example, royalties), the imbalance of power is skewed toward the universities as employers. Rhoades and Slaughter (1991) studied one research university's processes in adopting a technology transfer policy and related intellectual property provisions. They illustrated how certain groups, particularly administrators, emphasized hierarchical structures as a means to remind faculty and other process participants of their ultimate authority. In addition, to further accentuate the authority and power divide, Rhoades and Slaughter observed differences in resource availability among the participants. For example, the administrators had staff at their disposal to carry out some of the work related to the policy construction, whereas faculty and other participants had no supporting personnel.

Similarly, changes in administrative roles and control over intellectual property may occur over time. Identifying the relational shift between the university and faculty, Slaughter and Rhoades (1993) traced the policy shifts over intellectual property at one state institution. Specifically, they examined state statutes, system rules, and institutional policies during three periods of intellectual property policies (that is, 1969, 1977, and 1988). They observed a shift in administrative roles and control over those three periods. For example, in the initial 1969 policy, the university stood as the primary, relevant authority over intellectual property. In 1977, the policy added the Board of Regents to the mix while simultaneously increasing the university's "control and discretion over faculty's commercially relevant work" (p. 297). By 1988, new references to the state statutes were incorporated into the policy. According to Slaughter and Rhoades, this change indicated the increasing control of the overarching entity, the state, over commercially related activities. The change from 1969 to 1988 represents a shift in control over research away from academics to the state, and differentiation among state employees became blurred.

The construction of university patent policies also raises questions about group representation and whether faculty represent the greater corporate body or a narrower interest in the larger body or a subgroup. Rhoades and Slaughter (1991) noted the differences among viewpoints in which multiple groups acted in their own interest. They highlighted the conflicts and power struggles among the various actors: administrators, faculty, committee members, subcommittee members, and system boards. Each operates to further its goals seemingly without regard for the others, and faculty in the sciences particularly appear to advance goals related to their overarching field's needs without consideration of faculty in other domains or fields of study.

The development of university patent policies also illustrates the mixed messages that interested parties may send in their efforts to promote multiple yet conflicting benefits. As Rhoades and Slaughter (1991) observed, faculty presented "multiple symbolic commitments that undercut each other" (p. 76), such as when they expressed the norms of open science but then proposed language to reward academic inventors financially. These conflicting messages might be the result of faculty concessions. That is, when the faculty realized that these patent policies would be in place no matter what, they sought to compromise so as not to be left out of any financial returns.

Likewise, the conflicting messages are observable over time as intellectual property policies in the same institution or system are followed. Based on a study about intellectual property policies constructed at one state institution,

Slaughter and Rhoades (1993) traced how the ideology behind the intellectual property policy shifted from 1969 to 1988. In 1969, commercial activity and ownership arrangements defaulted to whatever agreement was made. By 1977, the policy indicated that transferring ownership to for-profit groups would not serve the public interest and discouraged such activity. But the tone of the 1988 policy changed, and the "public interest was redefined to allow the transfer of technology and title to the private sector" (p. 294). Thus, the prospects of commercial activity became more accepted, and the lines between the private and public sectors became less distinguishable.

These studies signal a turn away from the professoriate's control over its work products and work environments. Slaughter and Rhoades' study (1993), for example, explained how in the 1969 policy, faculty could participate in an "invention solely on their own time." In 1977, the policy no longer provided such a proviso and only acknowledged the possibility that faculty could have created inventions "partly on their own time." By 1988, the language of faculty ownership was deleted, and "there was no recognition that faculty had time separate from and outside the control of the university" (p. 294). In short, the policy changes reflected the movement from a professor with autonomy to a professor who reported to an employer. Thus, the power struggles in these studies illustrate the inherent conflicts and expressions of competing interests that arise when negotiating institutional patent policies at colleges and universities.

Questions of Ownership: Academe Versus Industry

Inventions and other research work between the academic community (that is, universities and academic scientists) and industry are typically legally governed by contract law. Generally, parties connected with the work sign an agreement, which derives from the principal contract. For instance, the university may have a written contract with a company to study a chemical reaction. The relevant parties, such as the academic scientists in the lab, would also likely sign a contract that adheres to the primary agreement between the university and the company.

Because the parties are free to negotiate the terms of the contract, the precise negotiated terms of these contracts vary substantially. Terms incorporated into the agreements regarding the patent provisions may outline provisions for ownership of patent rights, right of first refusal to obtain licensing, type of licensing, royalty amounts, management of the invention, prepublication reviews of works related to the invention, publication delays (typically not longer than three to six months), conditions for follow-up studies, invention audits, periodic lab inspections, arrangements for payment of services, steps to address conflicts of interest, and procedures to deal with infringement violations such as arbitration proceedings (see Castagnera, Fine, and Belfiore, 2002; Maxwell, Turley, Warren, and Wright, 2003; Newberg and Dunn, 2002).

Like university patent policies, provisions governing patents in contracts between the university and industry also demonstrate power struggles (see, for example, Blumenthal, Campbell, Causino, and Louis, 1996; Blumenthal, Causino, Campbell, and Louis, 1996; Press and Washburn, 2000). As a result of these negotiations, industry sponsorship results in industry ownership. This point is not surprising because industry pays for the services and expects a return in the form of patent ownership and revenues that derive from the intellectual property ownership. Furthermore, Mello, Clarridge, and Studdert (2005) found that conflicts also arose over intellectual property matters after the signing of the contract. Based on a study of 107 medical schools that participated in clinical trials for industry, 30 percent of respondents reported disputes with industry sponsors over intellectual property even after the contract was signed.

Despite these studies, some argue that power is not limited to one party, and imbalance of power may in reality represent equal power when the terms of the contract are properly negotiated upfront (see, for example, Casey, 2004; Newberg and Dunn, 2002). Based on feedback from members in the University-Industry Partnership, which represents universities and industry,[10] Casey (2004) noted that intellectual property issues are one of the most significant barriers to university and industry collaborations. Because intellectual property serves as a major stumbling block toward moving forward on projects, the parties likely have more equal footing at the negotiation table during the outset. Therefore, the provisions on intellectual property may not be as one-sided as perceived to be between universities and industry. The level playing field might be because the contract itself dictates the terms and no default rules are derived from, say, employment contracts and student handbooks, which would favor one party over another. As additional evidence of perhaps a more equal balance of power between universities and industry, Newberg and Dunn (2002) examined a case study over the establishment of the Net-centricity Laboratory at the University of Maryland to understand the processes of contract negotiations, particularly with regard to patent provisions. They concluded that the university's negotiating power was not negligible, and the institution had the leverage to negotiate terms that the university deemed critical, such as terms for intellectual property.

Challenges over patents, whether for infringement or interference, take their toll, and large litigation costs are associated with litigation avoidance, preparation, and actual procedures.[11] Of course, the payoff can sometimes be high for colleges and universities. For instance, in July 2006, *Inside Higher Education* reported that a "biotechnology company has agreed to pay the University of Alabama System $25 million to settle a patent infringement lawsuit" (Lederman, 2006). The university sued Nektar Therapeutics, alleging that its founder, a former professor at the university's Huntsville campus, had used patents owned by the university to create technologies valued at nearly $200 million. Similarly, in 2004 the *Chronicle of Higher Education* reported that after "11 years of litigation, the University of Colorado Health Sciences Center will finally receive a $58.3-million patent-infringement judgment from Wyeth, now that the U.S. Supreme Court has declined to consider an appeal sought by the giant pharmaceutical company" (Blumenstyk, 2004, p. A28).

Chapter Summary

This chapter illustrated how the law drives academic inventions, facilitates commercialization, and arbitrates conflicts associated with the first two. First, the combination of patent law and other legislation drives academic inventions because they provide substantial incentives for universities to engage in the commercialization of patentable products and processes. Second, as a facilitator to this commercial enterprise, the law leads to technology transfer now that federally funded research may be commercialized. Third, in response to questions of patent ownership and contract negotiations, the law delineates the rights and conditions associated with conflicts over academic inventions and their commercialization, conflicts exacerbated by technological changes, particularly shifts in biotechnology.

Several questions must be resolved to figure out the ownership rights of university and inventor: Do the documents and other supporting materials indicate whether an expressed agreement, implied agreement, or shop rights exist? In what capacity was the inventor hired, that is, was she or he hired to invent? Did the inventor use any university resources? Although this legal analysis serves its role in deciphering the parties' rights, based on the literature, more likely than not the university maintains an institutional patent policy that directs the parties to rights and responsibilities over an invention, so the focus is typically on whether an expressed or implied agreement exists. The construction of agreements and institutional policies, however, generates a discussion about the degree of power plays. The literature reveals that the power differential between faculty and administrators likely diminishes professors' rights over intellectual property, and in some cases, a divide may exist among faculty who negotiate for their own interests, not the interests of the corporate body. The power differential appears less significant between universities and industry so long as the negotiated terms are clear upon signing of the agreement.

Patents and Higher Education's Entry into the Market

S EVERAL FORCES CONTRIBUTED to the formation of a national innovation policy, and universities stood at the center of this policy development and implementation (Mowery, Nelson, Sampat, and Ziedonis, 2001; Nelson, 2001). A critical component of this national innovation policy movement included universities' participation in commercial activities (Pulsinelli, 2006). By doing so, universities and academic scientists were drawn to legal structures to protect their interests from encroachers who might hoard the invention and harm American innovation. For some inventors and universities, patents served as the best solution to protect these academic inventions from outside interference or infringement. But the seeking of patent protections does not come without controversy. A patent grants exclusive rights to the inventor or holder of the rights from others' use, sale, distribution, or production of the invention. These legal rights essentially establish a temporary monopoly over matters related to the invention and have been recognized as antithetical to the academic culture. To expand on these developments of the innovation agenda and choices of whether to patent academic research, this chapter discusses the forces that moved universities toward greater patent activities and explores the very arguments and interests related to university engagement in patent protections.

Development of University Patent Activities

The concept of commercializing academic research through patent activity started after a 1907 invention at Berkeley. At that time, Frederick Cottrell of the University of California patented his electrostatic precipitator, a device that removed particles from the air. His invention and subsequent patent sparked attention in higher education because it initiated the commercialization of academic research (Metlay, 2006; Mowery and Sampat, 2001a, 2001b). Further, after rolling out his invention in 1912, Cottrell established the Research Corporation, a patent management organization that relieves inventors from tackling the bureaucracy associated with the patent process. These events marked the start of a new era: commercialization of academic research.

The role of government also expanded around the conclusion of World War II (Geiger, 1986, 1993, 2004). During that time, a national report spurred conversation about government's advancement of science. Specifically, in 1945 Vannevar Bush proposed the idea that the government should stimulate scientific research to fight diseases, protect the nation, and support the public. To meet these goals, he recommended that the federal government invest in scientific talent and relinquish control over governmentally sponsored research to industry and universities. Berneman (2003) characterized this report as the application of the reservoir theory, a concept in which the federal government would subsidize basic research at universities and universities would thereby advance science with a reservoir of knowledge. In return, industry would transform the knowledge into commercial technology. Yet selected members of Congress and public officials at federal agencies questioned whether the government should engage in commercial activities and what role university-government projects would have in commercial ventures (Etzkowitz, Webster, Gebhardt, and Terra, 2000). Equally important, many universities behaved cautiously because governmental support could translate into governmental interferences (Price, 1954; Sanger, 1984, 1985). Despite these concerns, the federal government adopted Vannevar Bush's policy proposal and moved forward with subsidies for scientific research.

With increasing scientific research funding from the federal government, academic scientists could carry out their role as reservoirs of knowledge and explore critical national scientific policies such as space studies, drug treatments, and agricultural approaches. In addition, patenting of academic research started to grow from the late 1960s through the 1970s, when selected federal agencies permitted ad hoc determinations over whether universities could retain intellectual property rights of federally funded research (see, for example, Henderson, Jaffe, and Trajtenberg, 1998; Mowery, Nelson, Sampat, and Ziedonis, 2001). In 1968, the U.S. Department of Health, Education, and Welfare (HEW) formulated an institutional patent agreement so that universities could request filing of patents for academic research products and processes developed with HEW funds (Metlay, 2006; Mowery and Sampat, 2001a, 2001b; Mowery and Ziedonis, 2002). Following that policy change, university patents from governmentally sponsored projects increased substantially during the 1970s (Mowery and Sampat, 2001a, 2001b). With the growth, Mowery and Sampat (2001a) noted, many universities began to move away from using external brokers like Research Corporation and instead developed university patent and licensing offices. In fact, in the 1970s high research productive universities such as Boston University, California Institute of Technology, Colorado State, Cornell, Georgia, Harvard, Iowa, Johns Hopkins, Stanford, Southern California, and Virginia established patent and licensing operations (Association of University Technology Managers, 2007). These factors contributed to the increases in university patents.

Although specific federal agencies' intellectual property agreements and the growth in the number of university patent and licensing offices facilitated the increases in the number of university patent activities, it was passage of the Bayh-Dole Act in 1980 (35 U.S.C. §200, et seq. (2008)) that represented the single monumental event for the commercialization of federally supported academic research (Gulbrandsen, 2007). This legislation permitted universities to patent federally funded research, a policy that was not uniformly applied by many federal funding agencies until 1980.

The Bayh-Dole Act

Officially known as the Patent and Trademark Act Amendments of 1980, this legislation, which was authored by Senators Birch Bayh of Indiana and Bob Dole of Kansas and enacted on December 12, 1980, permits universities to hold the patent rights and corresponding license revenue from federally funded projects. Before passage of the Bayh-Dole Act, only selected federal agencies participated in institutional patent agreements with universities. Furthermore, treatment of intellectual property differed even in a federal agency and its contract with a university. The Bayh-Dole Act established a uniform system for intellectual property over federally funded research to nonprofit universities. Specifically, the law provides for the following applications to federally funded research:

A uniform patent agreement with federal agencies;

An opportunity for nonprofit organizations, including universities, to file for patent protections of discoveries and inventions;

A reward system for inventors, which includes sharing proceeds;

A nonexclusive license to the federal government;

"March-in" rights (or access) to technology not used for commercial activities;

A mandate that discoveries and licenses remain in the United States; and

Rights of universities holding the patent to assign exclusive licenses to the technology.

The law formally established another opportunity for universities to qualify for an additional interest from federally subsidized projects.

Accordingly, university patent activity increased significantly after the passage of the Bayh-Dole Act (Dai, Popp, and Bretschneider, 2005). In the decade before the passage of the Bayh-Dole Act, the U.S. Patent and Trademark Office issued fewer than four hundred U.S. patents each year to the universities that represented the top one hundred institutions in research and development (National Science Board, 1993). By 1985, the number of patents issued to these institutions soared to 587, and by 1991, more than thirteen hundred patents were issued to these institutions (see Figure 2). Furthermore, during fiscal year 2006, the U.S. Patent and Trademark Office issued more than thirty-two hundred patents to the 189 member institutions of the Association of University Technology Managers, which are primarily universities (Association of University Technology Managers, 2007). Put simply, the Bayh-Dole Act contributes to the heightened interest about university patents.

Upon the law's enactment, many touted that it nearly single-handedly accelerated higher education's participation in commercial enterprises and

FIGURE 2

U.S. Patents Awarded to the 100 Academic Institutions with the Greatest R&D Volume: 1972–1991

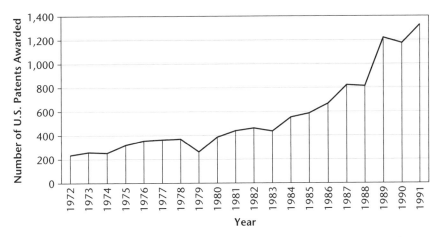

Source: Authors' depiction of NSF data on patents awarded to U.S. universities (National Science Board, 1993).

patent activities (see, for example, Ramirez, 2004). Although in practice this law may not have accomplished as much as is attributed to it (Boettiger and Bennett, 2006; Nelson, 2001), the law appealed to many universities that sought to patent academic research, and it serves as a reminder of academic research's commercial potential through patenting and licensing activities. Thus, at the very least, the law advanced its purpose of commercializing research and spurring on technological innovation through patent and licensing activities at American universities.

Expansion of Patentable Subject Matter

Also in 1980, a landmark case that emerged from research advancements further defined what qualified as patentable subject matter. In *Diamond* v. *Chakrabarty,* the Supreme Court held that a genetically manufactured microorganism qualified as a patentable subject matter. To arrive at its decision, the Court broadly construed the meaning of patentable subject matter in the patent statute, which gives patent protection to "any new and useful process, machine, manufacture, or composition of matter" (p. 307). Additionally, the Court examined the legislative history of patent law and concluded that "Congress intended statutory subject matter to 'include anything under the sun that is made by man'" (p. 309). Consistent with that decision, patent examiners and the federal courts adopted a more expansive determination of what qualified as patentable subject matter. In fact, later that year the U.S. Patent and Trademark Office issued a patent for a gene cloning process, which surprised many when it occurred (Demaine and Fellmeth, 2002; Dillen, 1997).

In addition to the inclusion of biotechnology in the scope of patentable subject matter and processes, the U.S. Patent and Trademark Office included electronic technology in the scope of patentable inventions. Indeed, in the late 1990s, computer technology using specially defined algorithms became recognized as patentable subject matter (see *State Street Bank and Trust Co. v. Signature Financial Group,* 1998). Basically, as technological advancements occurred, judicial and federal agency interpretations expanded the scope of patentable subject matter. This broadening of the patentable subject matter opened more opportunities for universities to patent new academic research and resulted in more patent filings (Mowery, Nelson, Sampat, and Ziedonis, 2001).

Technology Transfer

With the events described, the interest over the commercialization of academic research increased substantially after 1980 (Seeley, 2003). Universities began to engage in "technology transfer," the process to convert research knowledge and findings into commercial products or processes, which in turn establishes patenting and related intellectual property activities such as licensing and marketing. As technology transfer became a more recognized practice, universities formed technology transfer offices with the express intent to commercialize academic research through patenting and licensing. In the 1980s, the higher education community observed the establishment of technology transfer programs at large research universities such as Arizona State, Case Western, Dartmouth, Duke, Emory, Florida, Illinois, North Carolina State, Oregon State, Purdue, and Washington (Association of University Technology Managers, 2007).

Today, although most university patents do not generate enough income to cover sufficiently the operating costs (Powers, 2006), research activities are pursued with an eye toward potential financial rewards. Not surprisingly when university patents are mentioned, academics and the lay public think in terms of the big patent winners. For instance, the literature and media discussions often refer to Gatorade (University of Florida) and the search engine Google (Stanford University). But other major products and processes connected with university patents also play a major role in the market—Carnegie Mellon's search engine Lycos; Emory's Atripla, the single tablet for HIV patients; Florida State's anticancer drug Taxol; and the University of Florida's cellulosic waste processing to produce more efficient forms of ethanol. Less well known but very successful university patents include the University of Washington's interactive simulation of legislative and electoral politics known as LegSim.

In sum, an interactive development has occurred between patent law and policy, technological advancements, and competing interests which shape intellectual property policies and practices for colleges and universities. Given these developments, universities could hardly resist the movement toward patents. Yet these movements have not come without controversy and critique.

Debates About University Patent Activities

The national system of innovation encouraged university participation in advancing technology transfer (Mowery, Nelson, Sampat, and Ziedonis, 2001; Nelson, 2001), but studies have expressed differing conclusions about whether universities should engage in the commercialization of research through patenting. Proponents of university patents argue that intellectual property enables academic scientists and universities to support knowledge flow and benefits to the public. Opponents of university patents argue that intellectual property limits access and allows one party to dictate the direction of that invention, which is antithetical to the academic culture and scientific inquiry.

Supporting University Patents
The literature presents four reasons to support university patenting of inventions over other entities: acknowledgment of the inventors, control of the

invention quality, accessibility to the invention, and a mission and goals aligned with the public interest.

First, university patents acknowledge the inventors (Campbell and Slaughter, 1999). Patents provide proper attribution of those significantly engaged in the invention's conception and development (Bagley, 2006; Patel, 1996). In particular, the patent process recognizes listed inventors through a national recording process that appears in the public record. In addition, upstream technologies (that is, new inventions based on knowledge from an earlier invention) often require citations of earlier patents, and these patent references attribute the patent application invention to earlier works. Furthermore, even if a university requires an inventor's assignment of patent rights (that is, to transfer the inventor's rights to the employer), the patent still identifies the inventor or inventors. Because financial rewards may be negligible for many inventions, attribution serves as a symbolic reward to the inventor, which in turn meets the intended policy purpose of creating incentives for creators and discoverers of academic inventions.

Second, university patents enable universities to control the invention's quality (Apple, 1989, 1996; Metlay, 2006; Mowery and Sampat, 2001a). As Apple (1989) noted, when Professor Harry Steenbock discovered the fortification process for Vitamin D while at the University of Wisconsin, one of the reasons that he patented his discovery was to control the product's quality. For him, the patent protection ensured control over the manufacturing process, which for Steenbock translated into manufacturing integrity. Similarly, Metlay (2006) illustrated an example in which another Wisconsin inventor who was also Steenbock's mentor, Stephen Babcock, did not patent his invention. The lack of control resulted in the distribution of poor-quality products. Besides the problems faced by retail consumers, the quality control problem could jeopardize the reputation of the university and the inventor. Thus, university patents permit some degree of control for the inventor.

Third, university patents typically allow for greater access to these inventions (Campbell, Powers, Blumenthal, and Biles, 2004; Kesselheim and Avorn, 2005; Pressman and others, 2006). In a study of DNA licensing at nineteen of the top thirty universities, many respondents indicated rather complex licensing schemes that closed survey responses do not factor. In particular, other studies on licensing did not reveal that exclusive licenses issued by the university sometimes include a humanitarian exception. The incorporation of these clauses suggests that universities might serve as better conductors of innovation than industry.

Similarly, academic scientists, by the nature of their professional culture, are more inclined to avail the invention to a greater scope of users (Ramirez, 2004; see also Hermanowicz, 1998). Under a university patent, the academic community is less likely to operate in a manner that monopolizes the invention and strictly controls the licensing practices of others to drive price controls and other unethical practices (Apple, 1996; Metlay, 2006). In fact, Professor Harry Steenbock's decision to patent his vitamin D discovery in 1924 was his effort to avoid "extortionate charges" that could potentially result from private industry if a company held the patent (Apple, 1989, p. 377; see also Metlay, 2006). Furthermore, universities are not likely candidates of technological suppression (Kesselheim and Avorn, 2005; Schacht, 2006). Accordingly, Ramirez (2004) suggested that patenting research tools, particularly by universities, might spur the downstream product development rather than result in an "anticommons" effect (see also Kesselheim and Avorn, 2005, for discussions of upstream patents).

Fourth, in furtherance of research for the public good, university engagement in patent activities fits its mission and roles better than other organizations, even other public service entities such as the government (Kesselheim and Avorn, 2005; Pressman and others, 2006). As Eisenberg (1996) noted, the government is not in business to commercialize (that is, to participate in patent and licensing activities). Universities are a better fit to serve as keepers of inventions, however, because they tend to share inventions, as demonstrated by the data on humanitarian licensing activities for basic research and research tools.

Opposing University Patents

Robert Merton's early works (1968, 1973) described the key features of scientific work, specifically that of scientific communalism, which involves the shared and open nature of scientific research. Patenting, however, involves the ownership and control over inventions. Consequently, patents transform the scientific norm of open access to a norm of proprietary interest (Metlay, 2006). This shift away from a sphere of communal use raises several arguments against university patenting activities. Opponents of university patenting argue that intellectual property in academic science alters scientific norms of openness, which alters the environment for academic-scientific work (Heller and Eisenberg, 1998; Rai, 1999; see generally Stein, 2004). The principal message in opposition of university patents thus rests on the theme of the anticommons. The following discussion elaborates on five reasons to oppose university patent activities as presented in the literature.

First, patents run counter to universities' public service role. According to these critics, the commercialization or privatization of academically created knowledge and goods specifically violates universities' public service role (Metlay, 2006; Palmer, 1934). In particular, if universities serve the public, their research should be free and readily accessible, and universities should not financially benefit from those inventions. In particular, Metlay (2006) and Palmer (1934) emphasized the inherent conflict with the university service role and financial rewards for medical inventions, including medicines and instruments.

Consistent with that stance, Harvard and Johns Hopkins Universities in 1934 discouraged patenting research findings unless such protection served the public good to avoid blocked access of the invention (Palmer, 1934). That position changed around the 1970s, however, when the two universities established technology transfer offices with significant patenting and licensing responsibilities, especially for medical products and processes (see also Mowery and Sampat, 2001b; Sampat, Mowery, and Ziedonis, 2003). Despite those earlier positions, the numbers may illustrate more concretely how these two universities changed their positions and subsequently became active participants in patent activities. In fiscal year 2006, Harvard received thirty-five U.S. patents, applied for 167 patents, and reported more than $20.8 million in license income (Association of University Technology Managers, 2007). Also in 2006, Johns Hopkins received eighty-two U.S. patents, applied for 329 patents, and reported more than $13.9 million in license income (Association of University Technology Managers, 2007). Simply put, the public service rhetoric changed substantially from the early 1900s to the present (Metlay, 2006).

Second, patents encourage at least two forms of data blockage: the withholding of data and the secrecy of academic research. For many academic scientists, such behaviors are linked to the commercialization of research and to the competition among the scientific community to receive inventor status. As inventor status follows a priority system (that is, the first inventor to give notice through a patent or publication holds the property rights), academic scientists have an interest to restrict, delay, or block scientific knowledge through such mechanisms as patenting (Campbell and others, 2002; Cohen and Walsh, 2007). Cohen and Walsh (2007) found that academic scientists do disclose required information related to patent descriptions and validation of the invention, but they question the extent to which academic scientists disclosed steps and other relevant data not required for disclosures yet pertinent to scientific progress.

This secrecy increases with industry involvement (see, for example, Bagley, 2006; Blumenthal and others, 1986; Blumenthal, Campbell, Causino, and Louis, 1996; Campbell, Louis, and Blumenthal, 1998; Hall, Link, and Scott, 2003). For example, in a 1985 survey of biotechnology faculty from the top forty universities in terms of federal research funds, respondents with industry funding were four times more likely than others to classify works as trade secrets (Blumenthal and others, 1986). A subsequent study in 1995 of 2,052 life science faculty from the top fifty universities that received funding from the National Institutes of Health also concluded that faculty involvement with industry significantly increased the likelihood of classifying works as trade secrets (Blumenthal, Campbell, Causino, and Louis, 1996). Consistent with those findings, Thursby and Thursby (2002) also concluded that industry agreements contributed to delays in publishing.

In addition to the tactic of limiting data sharing to protect one's interest for eventual commercial activity, the data access may result in an effort to keep inventions from patent and license activities. Based on a survey conducted in 1996–1997 of 3,804 medical faculty from 117 institutions, 2,366 faculty (62.2 percent response rate) responded to inquiries regarding data access to academic research (Campbell, Weissman, Causino, and Blumenthal, 2000). Among the key findings, the authors reported an increased likelihood that respondents would not share data with faculty who maintain high commercial activities. According to the authors, "Some scientists are reluctant to share their research results with commercially active investigators for fear that the shared data will be used for commercial rather than academic purposes" (Campbell, Weissman, Causino, and Blumenthal, 2000, p. 310).

Third, because patents require declaration of an invention's useful or practical purpose, the movement toward more university patents encourages applied research over basic research (Nelson, 2002). The Bayh-Dole Act, which encourages universities to engage in patent research for commercial use, exacerbates this priority on commercialization of academic research. As Landes and Posner (2003) cautioned, research done "to earn substantial income from patent licensing has, it appears, induced universities to substitute away from basic research, and the result may have been a net social loss" (p. 316). These activities encourage a shift away from basic research to applied research (but see Trajtenberg, Henderson, and Jaffe, 2002, who found that university patent holders still engaged in basic research). Nelson (2002) and others (for example, Lieberwitz, 2003, 2005) argued that economic incentives and legal policies favored commercial activity and most likely shifted academic research toward more applied areas. Indeed, two studies found that the choice of academic scientists' topics was significantly influenced by their commercial value (Blumenthal and others, 1986; Blumenthal, Campbell, Causino, and Louis, 1996; Walsh, Cho, and Cohen, 2005).

Fourth, inventions with multiple patents require so many layers of licensing approvals that they severely inhibit and stifle scientific progress, and university patents are not immune to this effect. Several have argued that multiple patents required for an invention complicated the research process because the barriers to patenting scientific studies were onerous (Clarkson and DeKorte, 2006; Heller and Eisenberg, 1998; Shapiro, 2000). As such, they serve as disincentives to pursue research.

Similar to universities' argument about their public service role, some have argued that a problem arises when researchers must overcome multiple patents from various patent holders to conduct a study (see, for example, Clarkson and DeKorte, 2006; Heller and Eisenberg, 1998; Kesselheim and Avorn, 2005; Shapiro, 2000). "When multiple organizations each own individual patents that are collectively necessary for a particular technology, . . . their competing intellectual property rights form a 'patent thicket'" (Clarkson and DeKorte, 2006, p. 181). Patent thickets require lengthy licensing approvals from each patent holder, and depending on the thoroughness and accuracy of the licensing approval process, the end user might be subject to an infringement action. Although articles about the patent thicket do not specifically address university patents, they illustrate a reason why university patents should not be sought: university patents would simply contribute to the patent thicket problem, which in turn represents anticommons behavior (see, for example, Clarkson and DeKorte, 2006; Heller and Eisenberg, 1998; Shapiro, 2000).

Fifth, university patent activities pass new, additional costs onto higher education and the public (de Larena, 2007). The literature overwhelmingly reports that technology transfer as measured through patents and licensing occurs at a loss (see, for example, Powers, 2006; Thursby and Thursby, 2003). Equally important, universities cannot afford to patent every invention. A university patent office must assess the potential value of the invention in light of its expected costs. Based on interviews with members of nineteen of the thirty academic institutions with the highest number of DNA patents, respondents indicated that "patent prosecution, maintenance, and management costs" for DNA patents would amount to approximately $20,000 to $30,000 per patent (Pressman and others, 2006). Indeed, a significant portion of those costs includes legal fees associated with filing the patent. According to the Association of University Technology Managers (2005), 191 of the association's members reported $221 million in expenditures for legal fees in 2004. Of that amount, only $91 million (41.3 percent) of their expenditures were reimbursed. Patenting and licensing activities represent significant expenses in the process.

Like the patent thicket problem (that is, licensing and approvals require multiple patent holders), Heller and Eisenberg (1998) argue, inflated costs from granting licensing to patents result in "stacking licenses" (that is, multiple licenses required to conduct research). These costs may inhibit the invention's progress. Furthermore, the patent thicket problem becomes more pronounced when the government underwrites the research. When the government pays for the research, the argument for public access strengthens; that is, because the public already paid for the research through tax dollars, everyone should have access to the works, and patents only prevent that access (Heller and Eisenberg, 1998). Consequently, as Heller and Eisenberg (1998) indicated, any additional costs to use the invention create economic "rents" paid to the holder of the patent. Simply put, costs associated with patenting serve as additional barriers to the goals of communal science.

Chapter Summary

This chapter traced the development of American higher education's commodification of knowledge and research products. At the core of U.S. innovation policy, universities were charged with the responsibility to invent and disseminate new creations for the public, which in turn reflected commercial purposes. The shaping of this policy operated with three significant triggers. First, universities and members of the academic community recognized their participation in patentable activities. For proponents of university patents, the intellectual property right acknowledged the first creators as inventors, enabled quality control over the inventions, provided greater accessibility to the inventions relative to what industry behaviors would follow, and supported higher education's mission to serve the public interest. Second, by 1980 with passage of the Bayh-Dole Act, universities gained patent rights over governmentally sponsored research. In other words, universities received a greater incentive to move inventions to market. Consequently, universities emphasized the commercialization of academic research products and processes. Furthermore, like many other situations in higher education, the legal structure opened the door for expressions of new preferences and interests, and bargaining, balancing, and leveraging took place (see also Pusser, 2004; Sun and Permuth, 2007). Third, as technology advanced, research increased. Equally important, technology forced changes to what became acceptable patentable subject matter. This change expanded the scope of patentable products and processes, particularly in the biotechnology field, which maintains a significant academic presence. Of course, this patent progress and U.S. policy innovation also come with drawbacks (Geiger, 2004; Heller and Eisenberg, 1998). Universities' assertion of intellectual property rights runs counter to their public service role, encourages data blockages and secrecy, rewards applied research over basic research, creates many layers for licensing approvals that severely inhibit or stifle scientific progress, and results in additional costs for the public to access the invention. In other words, university patent activities potentially support knowledge flow to benefit the higher education community and the public, and they potentially restrict knowledge flow by hindering research progress in the higher education community and the public but retain benefits at the individual or unit organizational levels.

Shared and Related Concerns About Intellectual Property

THE LAWS OF PATENTS AND COPYRIGHTS contain shared and related concerns about other legal issues pertaining to intellectual property. First, intellectual property includes more than the laws of patents and copyright. It also includes trademarks, trade names, and trade secrets. As the economic, political, and social forces set the stage, the legal parameters, technological advancements, and actor-based interests further define college and university policies and practices regarding trademarks, trade names, and trade secrets. For example, what is truly at stake when an unauthorized party uses a college's logo? How do universities protect their research secrets from industry and other educational institutions? What rights do universities have if an independent company uses references to their mascots in connection with its Web address or the corporate name (for example, Badger Inn and Suites, Bruin Brewery, Buckeye Industries)?

Second, the sources for these property rights—patents, copyrights, trademarks, trade names, and trade secrets—are not limited to the federal statutes. Although many refer to these respective laws as the source of legal parameters, other laws also govern the treatment of intellectual property, especially sovereign immunity. How does sovereign immunity alter the conditions of use and protection of intellectual property rights? What do these differences represent for higher education?

Third, we examine the role of the international setting to describe common characteristics of treaties pertaining to intellectual property, compliance with the international treaties, and a brief discussion about the comparative literature on higher education institutions' international policies and practices.

Trademarks and Trade Secrets

Unlike copyright and patent law, the law of trademarks and trade secrets does not expressly derive from the U.S. Constitution. Nevertheless, it represents significant legal protections over intellectual property, and for higher education, it symbolizes more obviously colleges' and universities' behaviors that resemble a business that attempts to protect its intellectual capital. Given the increasing competition for higher education and particularly the importance of college athletics, colleges and universities are increasingly involved in producing trademarks and trade names.[12] The institutions' involvement in technology transfer also creates the need for trade secrets. A trade secret, however, allows an organization to prevent disclosure of information that gives it a competitive edge over others. Thus, a trade secret protects information, while a trademark protects a distinctive name, design, logo, slogan, or other mark that identifies the organization and distinguishes it from others.

Trademarks

Trademarks are words, names, symbols, or devices used to distinguish and identify businesses, their products, or their processes to the general public. The trademark may be applied to T-shirts, hats, brochures, key chains, Web sites, Internet addresses, blog names, and names of organizations, including nonprofit entities (Lattinville, 1996; Manas, 2003)—as well as caskets (Troop, 2008). The first to use the "mark" owns it; however, to qualify for federal protection, the party must file the trademark with the U.S. Patent and Trademark Office.

To qualify for protection, the mark must be distinctive. A trademark is not limited to use of the college or university's name or logo. It may be the name, word, symbol, or device that signals a curriculum program, educational process, research project, event on campus, or residence hall, but it must be sufficiently distinctive from other potential marks or carry a secondary meaning that the consuming public likely associates with that product or process (Bearby and Siegal, 2002; Lattinville, 1996). Several decades ago, the New Jersey Institute of Technology created the name "Virtual Classroom" and registered the name for federal trademark protection when it established an educational program for students to learn from outside the traditional brick-and-mortar format (Blumenstyk, 1998).

Trademarks are covered by federal law under the Lanham Act. In addition, states also have laws that protect unauthorized use of trade names and trademarks. In fact, owners of trademarks and trade names may sue unauthorized users under multiple sources of law to maximize the potential for obtaining jurisdiction over the defendants and seeking legal remedies. The reasons for granting exclusive rights to trademarks originally stemmed from the logic of protecting the public from being deceived, but more recently, their protection stems from the justification that unauthorized users do not undermine the rights of trademark owners through misappropriations or illegal uses of brand names (Doellinger, 2007). Recent treaties also offer relative global protection of trademarks (Leaffer, 1998).

Trademark law applies generally to commercial entities, but many institutions of higher education can and do assert trademarks for at least three interrelated reasons. First, institutions wish to protect their names and reputations, and their names and symbols distinguish one organization from another (Manas, 2003). Johnson (2006) argues that proliferation of unaccredited online degree programs and fake institutions and practices, such as diploma mills' maintaining names resembling existing colleges and universities, raises concerns about consumer protection. For example, Johnson (2006) notes the similarity between the name of Trinity Southern University, a diploma mill, and Trinity University, "a reputable accredited school in San Antonio, Texas" (p. 445). Based on reputational concerns, Trinity University sought a permanent injunction to stop Trinity Southern University from using the name "Trinity." The court granted the injunction because the name, Trinity Southern University, was too close and would create confusion with the established Trinity University.

In 1999, Ohio University and the Ohio State University also settled a trademark dispute, but oddly enough, it was about the use of the word "Ohio" ("Ohio U. and Ohio State U. Settle Trademark Tussle over 'Ohio'," 1999). Ohio University registered the word, and a dispute soon arose with Ohio State. The agreement negotiated acceptable uses of the word *Ohio*, so it would not create confusion for the public.

Second, colleges and universities recognize the direct financial benefits associated with protecting their trademarks (Lattinville, 1996). In particular, lucrative athletic activities have led colleges and universities to protect their financial interests in their logos, names, products, and mascots. Many universities have established licensing offices to protect their trademarks and to exploit them for commercial gain. In 2006, the University of Texas reached the highest levels for collegiate licensing royalties with estimates of revenues at around $90 million (Palaima, 2006). Although most institutions report small fractions of this amount such as the University of Kansas' estimate of about $1 million annually from trademark licensing revenues (Aronauer, 2005), trademarks and licensing of the trademarks still generate revenues to subsidize athletics or other administrative units (Phillips, 2007).

Third, universities, particularly those engaged in commercial activities, may use trademarks to protect their products, processes, or traditions. For example, universities engaged in inventing pharmaceutical drugs may have to contend with trademark and patent laws. The production of drugs can also implicate trade secrets. Similarly, Brown, Zuefle, and Batista (2007) trace the brand equity significance of a historical event to one university. The authors describe the dispute between Texas A&M University and the professional football Seattle Seahawks over references to "the twelfth man." Texas A&M claimed rights to references about the twelfth man. Based on a crucial football game in 1922, the Texas A&M coach asked a player, E. King Gill, to suit up because the team was running low on reserve players and he might be needed. Texas A&M won the game and beat the then top team in the nation. Although Gill never played in the game, he was available as the twelfth player in the event he was needed. Because the Seattle Seahawks would not stop using references to the twelfth man, Texas A&M initiated a lawsuit that was eventually settled; however, the case symbolizes the significance of brand equity and control over historical references to one university. Similarly, Princeton University sued Trenton State College in 1996 when the latter changed its name to the College of New Jersey. Princeton had been incorporated and was known as the College of New Jersey until 1896. The lawsuit was settled when both colleges agreed to make clear that each has a separate history ("Princeton Settles Suit," 1996).

Simply put, a college or university's trademark signifies a mark with reputational and economic values. An institution's trademark represents the brand equity, so protection has become essential for control, attribution, use, and reward. It places efforts to distinguish itself from other organizations to avoid confusion, avoid reputational harm, and ensure revenues associated with the trademark.

Trade Secrets

Trade secrets represent protected information in the form of formulas, patterns, devices, techniques, processes, or compilations. Through legal protection as trade secrets, owners maintain competitive advantages over those who do not know the information. By definition, trade secrets do not exist if the information is copyrighted, patented, or otherwise properly "known." Generally speaking, trade secrets protect information that attaches some economic value, whether definitively realized or not, and warrant reasonable reasons to block others from having the information (David, 1993).

Unlike other intellectual property, which enjoys federal laws for protection, protection of trade secrets varies from state to state. Most states, however, have adopted the Uniform Trade Secrets Act, thus ensuring relative uniformity in defining trade secrets and misappropriations of those protected secrets among the adopting states. Trade secrets have been brought closer to patents and copyrights by technological developments and recent history of litigation, as information that is kept secret can be a source of income (David, 1993).

In the context of higher education, trade secrets do not present as major a concern as patents and copyrights; however, as institutions and faculty look to private sources for funding research, the private interests of those sources begin to shape what happens in universities—which includes the increasing focus on protection of trade secrets. Faculty and students may be required to maintain secrecy over the results of research, for example, thus creating conflicts between their and private entities' economic interests in keeping secrets to maintain their competitive advantages and their academic interests in making ideas freely accessible. University-industry collaborations present particularly difficult dilemmas in this regard (see, for example, Blumenthal and others, 1986; Newberg and Dunn, 2002). For instance, a chemistry professor at Wayne State misappropriated protected information that a chemist in New England classified as a trade secret (Blumenstyk, 1994, 1995). The protected information revealed a chemical composition that would glow at the presence of selected diseases in human bodies. Rather than complying with the nondisclosure of the trade secret, the professor used the information, patented it, and created a spin-off company. Later, he was sued, and Wayne State was required to surrender its interest in the company.

The reasons for protecting trade secrets may also serve the interests of the public. Protecting trade secrets potentially provides academics—particularly academic scientists—more time to study an issue such as a process, drug, or technique before placing it on the market. The more in-depth studies may prevent unintended consequences or unknown variables related to the product or process that with time may be uncovered. The university's corporate partner, however, may wish to roll out the product or process quickly to establish itself in the market.

Although attempts to maintain secrecy in research occur in higher education, certain instances present possible limits to asserting nondisclosure under protection of trade secrets, which may discourage industry interactions (Shockley, 1994). For public institutions, laws requiring open records and open meetings may, for all practical purposes, preclude trade secrets. Shockley (1994) concludes that state sunshine laws, particularly state open record laws, likely require disclosure of research documents and other related documents at public institutions. Blumenstyk (1991) reports that a public institution's decision to classify research information as a trade secret does not always mean that the information qualifies as a trade secret. Based on a lawsuit decided by the North Carolina Court of Appeals, animal activists could receive data about the University of North Carolina's research that involved the use of animals.

Similarly, disclosure of data on projects that involve federal agencies or federal grants is not necessarily protected as a trade secret. Except in cases of premature data or entanglement with national security, information involving federal agencies or federal grants falls under the Freedom of Information Act (5 U.S.C. §552, et seq.), which also requires disclosure of federal documents. More important, the Data Access Amendment of 1999 in the Freedom of Information Act mandates public access to federally sponsored research data that grantees maintain (Wagner, 2005). Thus, trade secrets likely do not apply to projects that receive public funding.

The International Setting

Interests and infringements on intellectual property are not bound to the United States. Our global access to educational materials, expressions, ideas, and concepts extends beyond country boundaries (Dinwoodie and Okediji, 2004). Not surprisingly, the issues of intellectual property are becoming more pervasive as members of the academic community share resources and post original expressions on the Internet and in other media, colleges and universities increasingly become transnational organizations with campuses in multiple countries and online availability, and academic content continues to expand with the inclusion of global products and processes and permission required from overseas. Given these circumstances, international intellectual property issues are of particular concern to the higher education community.

For the signatory countries, international treaties typically establish three common guidelines, which shape intellectual property policies at U.S.-based colleges and universities. First, many of the international treaties establish minimum standards. The purpose of the minimum standards permits some consistency in protection policies throughout the signatories to the treaty. For example, the 1989 amendments to the Berne Convention for the Protection of Literary and Artistic Works establish copyright protections for fifty years beyond the author's death, except for photographic and cinematographic works, which follow different standards. Second, the international treaties typically require declared participants to carry out their laws under a principle of equal treatment. That is, creators of intellectual property who are outside the participating country are still eligible for the same rights as those in the participating country. For example, the Berne Convention, which is in force in the United States, permits writers, artists, and other creators of intellectual property who reside outside the United States to receive the same rights as copyright applicants who reside in the United States. Third, the treaties also attempt to harmonize international policies and procedures. Because a creator of intellectual property may desire protections from multiple countries, international treaties attempt to create harmony or common standards that reduce the complex nature of an applicant who seeks protection in multiple countries. For instance, the Patent Law Treaty, to which the United States acceded, establishes a standard form for international patent applications. Consequently, an applicant may easily establish patent rights in multiple countries that are signatories to the treaty with the use of the same form, or, in some cases, the applicant maintains substantially similar information among the signatory countries without having to file forms that require drastically different information.

Practically speaking, international treaties that pertain to intellectual property defer to the country at issue. Accordingly, compliance of intellectual property requires knowledge of the laws of the nation to which the right is being asserted or challenged. For the most part, legal parameters pertaining to intellectual property derive from the respective nation, and there are no per se international laws on intellectual property. In the United States, several federal laws, mentioned earlier in this monograph, craft the laws around intellectual property. In addition, selected state laws also serve as additional or related legal parameters to define intellectual property rights. In contrast, international treaties do not prescribe domestic laws as detailed legal parameters. Instead, compliance of international treaties simply refers to legal compliance of the nation that awards the intellectual property.

Besides compliance with international treaties, the literature pertaining to the process of international intellectual property provides more revealing insights about the forces and direct factors that shape intellectual property policies at U.S.-based colleges and universities. Over the past several decades, activity in international intellectual property laws has signaled significant changes in matters of trade and naturally followed concerns of industry. In particular, international dialogue in groups—especially the World Intellectual Property Organization, a United Nations office that oversees intellectual property matters—and participants of the Uruguay Round pushed for intellectual property treaties that centered on trade. In 1994, the Agreement on Trade-Related Aspects of Intellectual Property Rights (TRIPS) failed to even include critical groups such as higher education, libraries, and research centers in the draft. Okediji (2003) posited that the omission of these voices signaled international priorities. Basically, the "coalition preference suggests that the governments' interests in negotiating the TRIPS Agreement were more or less consistent with those of industry" (Okediji, 2003, p. 852). Consequently, one may argue that higher education does not meet the goals of the group; therefore, as a body, its opinion is not valued. An alternative argument is that higher education need not be differentiated from industry because higher education maintains the same private, commercially driven interests. Regardless of the actual intent, the outcome of TRIPS is to treat intellectual property as an industrial trade item, which does not appear inconsistent with the general message of commodifying knowledge, even in higher education.

Similarly, from an international perspective, the privatization of knowledge and its market effects have filtered into higher education institutions beyond the United States. For instance, Wilkinson (2000) examined intellectual property and national policies in Canada with regard to innovation and concluded that Canada's universities face conflicting messages. On the one hand, they display evidence of increasing commercialization of academic works with public funds, but on the other, they advocate public interest and openness to academic works. Similarly, in the context of trademarks, Reimertshofer (1997) compared U.S. trademark protections with German trademark law in the setting of collegiate trademarks and licensing, especially in light of a recent German Supreme Court opinion that permitted protections for German universities. Reimertshofer suggested that in light of Germany's reduced governmental support for higher education, universities may resort to finding alternative revenue streams like many public institutions in the United States, and trademark licensing income in Germany may follow some U.S. policies and practices.

The practices of intellectual property activity, especially technology transfer, also align with this perspective. According to a study conducted by Slaughter and Leslie (1997), which included institutions from Australia, the United Kingdom, and the United States, the forty-seven faculty members from eight different units reported the reason for tapping into new revenue streams was a "means to serve their unit, do science, and serve the common good" (p. 179). This quasi-altruism shifted the faculty identities as researchers "to define themselves as inventors and entrepreneurs," and their behaviors placed new emphasis on intellectual property rights, development, and marketing (Slaughter and Leslie, 1997, p. 179). Across the continents, faculty from each institution believed that if they did not participate with industry and governmental entities and build an understanding of economic development practices, they would lose control of their work environment. In essence, they compromised their positions slightly to avoid major changes in their profession entirely. According to Slaughter and Leslie (1997), these movements represent academic capitalism, the process of commodifying academic expertise.

Simply put, this body of literature conveys a global movement in which higher education institutions increasingly pursue commercial activities. The economic, political, and social forces along with more direct factors related to the legal, technological, and various competing interests contribute to the intellectual property policies and practices at colleges and universities, even internationally.

Sovereign Immunity

Sovereign immunity represents a crucial legal construct that furthers the privatization of knowledge, which intellectual property laws ensure. Sovereign immunity is a doctrine that permits a state actor or an entity deemed as an arm of the state from being sued without expressly authorizing suits on that subject matter. In very basic terms, it stands for the proposition that state entities cannot be sued. Because intellectual property primarily derives from federal law, the doctrine of sovereign immunity means that public institutions of higher education are not subject to certain provisions, specifically monetary damages owed from infringements of intellectual property. Consequently, this doctrine shifts the balance of power over intellectual property in favor of public institutions.

Rationale for Sovereign Immunity

The classic American statement of sovereign immunity was uttered by Justice Oliver Wendell Holmes in the 1907 case *Kawananakoa* v. *Polyblank*: "There can be no legal right against the authority that makes the law on which the right depends" (p. 353). In the case, a bank received partial proceeds from the foreclosure of a mortgage, but part of the land was exempted from the judgment because it had been conveyed to the territory of Hawaii. The bank wanted the proceeds from all the land, arguing that the territory of Hawaii was much like the District of Columbia, a municipal corporation subject to a civil lawsuit. The territory argued that it was sovereign and did not consent to be sued. Justice Holmes' opinion for the Supreme Court agreed with the territory.

The doctrine of sovereign immunity was codified in the Eleventh Amendment, which states, "The Judicial Power of the United States shall not be construed to extend to any suit in law or equity, commenced or prosecuted against one of the United States, by citizens of another state, or by citizens or subjects of any foreign state." The legal question of Eleventh Amendment law is to what extent a state (or its subdivisions, agencies, and officials) may be sued by a private citizen in federal court. The Eleventh Amendment seeks to preserve or restore the states' sovereign immunity, and it extends to the political bodies that can claim the status of "sovereignty." The courts have determined that political subdivisions of the state that are essentially "arms of the state" can claim immunity, as Congress cannot abolish state immunity under its authority to create laws. States can waive immunity, and they have done so in certain situations (for example, in negligence suits that involve a state actor's harming a person or entity); however, based on several U.S. Supreme Court cases, a state waives sovereign immunity only upon clear expressions of that waiver.[13] A number of reasons have been given for state immunity. First, the state treasury belongs to everyone, and it would be unfair to all if it were used to pay damages to particular individuals or institutions. The related concern here is that lawsuits against the state will flood the courts. Second, suits against the state prevent government officials from doing the jobs they are obligated to do, jobs that are in the public interest. Furthermore, one can sue officials who act outside the law, and enforcing, say, an unconstitutional statute is considered acting outside the law (*Ex parte Young,* 1908). Third, the state can waive its immunity if it deems it in the public interest. The notion behind this idea is that the state is a representative bureaucracy whose decisions are subject to change through the political process. At the root of the sovereign immunity doctrine is a fear of federal power, which is uniquely American.

Public/Private Colleges and Universities Distinguished

The sovereign immunity doctrine presents a legal conundrum for state entities such as public colleges and universities over the enforcement of monetary liability under federal intellectual property laws. Because the sovereign immunity doctrine permits states to block certain claims against state entities, this doctrine gives public institutions of higher education a legal advantage over private institutions in cases of intellectual property challenges. Private institutions would have to pay for intellectual property infringement, while public institutions often do not. For instance, the U.S. Court of Appeals for the Fourth Circuit held in *Richard Anderson Photography* v. *Brown* (1988) that Radford University, a public institution in Virginia, could not be sued for violating the Copyright Act of 1976. Radford University had contracted with a Baltimore company to produce a student prospectus. The company in turn contracted with Richard Anderson Photography (RAP) to provide photographs for use in Radford's student prospectus. RAP owned the copyrights to a large set of photographs, some of which were published in the prospectus in accordance with their contract. RAP then heard that Deborah Brown, the university's director of public relations, was using the photographs without authorization (apparently she was using them in brochures soliciting money for the Radford Athletic Association). RAP sued Radford University and Brown (in her individual capacity) for damages under the federal Copyright Act of 1976. Radford University and Brown sought to dismiss the case on Eleventh Amendment grounds, with Brown also claiming immunity under a state law permitting immunity for officials.

RAP argued that by passing the Copyright Act, Congress essentially abolished the states' sovereign immunity, or, conversely, that by using copyrighted materials, the state institution constructively waived its immunity. The court held that Radford University had immunity but that Brown did not. Radford University's immunity was upheld because the Copyright Act did not clearly and unequivocally show an intention by Congress to abolish Eleventh Amendment immunity, and participation in the activity governed by the statute did not constitute a waiver of immunity. The court here took as given that Radford University was a sovereign entity simply because it was a public institution, an assumption that most courts make. Furthermore, this case suggests that public institutions may infringe on others' intellectual property, even for their own economic (as opposed to academic) purposes, and the law will shield them. These institutions then gain a significant competitive advantage over private entities, including private colleges and universities.

Similarly, in a multiyear litigation involving the University of Houston, the U.S. Court of Appeals for the Fifth Circuit ruled that a university press at a public institution also qualified for sovereign immunity for copyright challenges (*Chavez* v. *Arte Publico Press,* 2000). In that case, Denise Chavez, a nationally renowned playwright and commentator on issues relating to Latinas, entered into a contract in 1984 with Arte Publico Press, a component of the University of Houston, for publication of her books. In 1986, the press published a first printing of *The Last of the Menu Girls,* a collection of Chavez's short stories, registering the copyright in Chavez's name as author and owner. Twice in later years, the parties agreed on additional publishing contracts for the book, but in 1992, Chavez, dissatisfied because the university had failed to correct errors in the earlier printings, refused to permit the university to print any more copies than agreed to in a 1991 contract. Around October 1992, however, the university informed Chavez that the 1991 contract did not limit the number of copies it could print and declared its intention to print five thousand more copies of the book.

Chavez's complaint alleges that the university and one of its officials infringed her copyright in her book. She sought a declaratory judgment securing her rights under the contract, damages, and an injunction against the university. The university moved to dismiss the suit on Eleventh Amendment grounds because it had sovereign immunity from intellectual property lawsuits. In light of a U.S. Supreme Court case decided in 1998, which reaffirmed that sovereign immunity could not be removed without the express authorization from a state, the U.S. Court of Appeals for the Fifth Circuit ruled in favor of the university based on sovereign immunity.

This case illustrates several points about the significance of sovereign immunity as a defense for public institutions in intellectual property lawsuits. First, it illustrates what now happens to lawsuits that seek damages for intellectual property infringement against public universities: generally speaking, those universities may infringe intellectual property of private individuals without fear of monetary liability. Second, even public university presses can now claim sovereign immunity, even though their actions have very little to do with governmental actions or even actions that are core to the university's purpose. Furthermore, although university presses function like a business with the hope of serving auxiliary functions of the state with a profit, it warrants sovereign immunity protections.

In light of the intellectual property activities and state institutions' defenses of intellectual property lawsuits under sovereign immunity, questions arise over the "public" nature of higher education and specifically public colleges and universities. For instance, in *BV Engineering* v. *University of California, Los Angeles* (1988), the plaintiff, BV Engineering—which manufactures and sells computer software products—sued UCLA for copyright infringement. UCLA purchased one copy each of seven computer programs, with the accompanying user manuals, but then made three copies of each program and ten copies of each manual. BV sued UCLA for copyright infringement, trademark infringement, and breach of contract under the Copyright Act of 1976. The U.S. Court of Appeals for the Ninth Circuit held for the university, indicating that the Copyright Act did not expressly abolish state immunity. This case illustrates the general trend that the copyright acts do not abolish state immunity because they do not do so expressly, despite language indicating that "anyone" who violates the acts is liable, and so public universities probably can freely violate copyrights. The Supreme Court would later make abolishing immunity in intellectual property cases extremely difficult, even when expressly done so in the law. It is clear also that public universities are becoming adept at using the courts to shield themselves from the laws. The University of California, in this case a defendant, is soon to become a major plaintiff in intellectual property cases, using intellectual property laws to further its economic goals, but when sued it resorts to its "publicness" to shield itself from those very laws.

Likewise, in *Genentech* v. *Regents of the University of California* (1998), Genentech appealed the dismissal of its case, seeking declaratory judgment that the university and Eli Lilly were violating its rights regarding a patent for producing human insulin. The U.S. Court of Appeals for the Federal Circuit indicated that to waive Eleventh Amendment sovereign immunity, a state must expressly waive those rights. At the end, the court ruled that the university consented to this suit through its voluntary, deliberate, and continuous litigation in this matter and its own charge of patent infringement raised in the case. More interesting to us here is the court's questioning of the university's purported "publicness," stating:

It is also a factor to be considered that the University's actions are not at the core of the educational/research purposes for which the University was chartered as an arm of the state, although the record contains no basis for disputing that a research university's patenting activity serves to move into public benefit scientific inventions that might otherwise languish as laboratory curiosities. . . . We too do not answer that question [of whether there may be some state instrumentalities that qualify as "arms of the state" for some purposes but not others], for our decision does not require analysis of the magnitude of the commercial component in the relationship between the University's research activities and its dissemination of that research through patents and industrial licenses. However, it is not irrelevant, in connection with the University's claimed immunity, that this commercially-oriented activity is not central to the University's charter [Genentech v. Regents of the University of California, 1998, pp. 1453–1454].

In short, a public college or university's actions may resemble a private firm, but in cases involving intellectual property challenges, it also holds the rights of public protection through the sovereign immunity doctrine.

Maneuvering Around Sovereign Immunity

A state agency, including a public college or university, may, however, waive its rights to sovereign immunity when the public institution initiates the action or makes claims toward rights of intellectual property over a product or process. In *New Star Lasers* v. *Regents of the University of California* (1999), the issue related to the university's disputed patent for the Dynamic Cooling Device (DCD) technology. This technology is useful in conjunction with a laser skin treatment process marketed by New Star Lasers (NSL). In 1994, the university and NSL attempted to negotiate the sale of a limited-use license for the DCD technology. The negotiations apparently proceeded only to an option agreement to continue exclusive negotiations, and the parties disputed whether or not NSL exercised that option. Meanwhile, a disagreement over the technology developed between the university and Candela Corporation, culminating an infringement action in federal court in Massachusetts, which the university ultimately settled by granting to Candela an exclusive license in the DCD technology, a settlement allegedly in conflict with the negotiations or agreements with NSL. Candela and NSL attempted to negotiate a license of their own but failed to reach agreement, and NSL subsequently filed suit against both Candela and the university. The university claimed Eleventh Amendment immunity. A federal district court held against the university, arguing that this case was not merely about an infringement, which would be barred by the Eleventh Amendment, but about the validity of the patent in question. Thus, amenability to a suit challenging the validity of a patent is an integral part of the patent scheme. The issue here is that the university was attempting to claim that questions about its patents can never be addressed, giving it not only a competitive edge over private entities in being shielded from infringement actions but even from challenges to patents themselves, which would essentially kill the patent system and allow state actors to shut out private ones.

Likewise, in *Vas-Cath, Inc.* v. *Curators of the University of Missouri* (2007), the University of Missouri initially filed as a patent interference hearing against Vas-Cath over patent rights associated with specially designed catheters to treat kidney failure. The federal trial court ruled in the University of Missouri's favor, and Vas-Cath appealed. On appeal of the decision, the university asserted sovereign immunity to block Vas-Cath from pursuing its appeal. The U.S. Court of Appeals for the Federal Circuit, which hears patent appeal cases, ruled that a state entity could not assert sovereign immunity after the state entity initiated and participated in the interference hearing.

Although the literature is bereft of discussions that address colleges' and universities' assertion of sovereign immunity over intellectual property challenges, Klein (2005) presents a detailed analysis of the legal strategies that might avail public institutions to lawsuits under federal copyright law despite defenses of sovereign immunity. Based on a legal analysis of case law and suggestions from constitutional law scholars who comment on sovereign immunity, Klein (2005) highlights the differences between public and private in legal treatment, but he suggests that lawsuits against public colleges and universities for copyright infringement are legitimate, as the U.S. Supreme Court declared patent laws subject only to sovereign immunity and not copyright law.

Furthermore, Klein notes that the Eleventh Amendment is not an absolute right and that avenues exist to initiate a federal copyright lawsuit against a state agency or individual state employee. For instance, he suggests that plaintiffs sue the state under the Fifth Amendment's Takings Clause. That is, the state is taking property owned by a citizen and experiences economic harm from such action.[14] In addition, he proposes that plaintiffs may sue the public institution employee personally. If accepted by the courts, this proposal would likely limit the use of copyrighted works, even those eligible for fair use, because public employees such as professors and other academic staff would likely air on cautionary measures. As established in the previous chapter, matters of fair use raise more questions than answers. Therefore, in light of the ambiguity on what constitutes fair use and the potential for public employees' personal liability for using copyrighted works, public colleges and universities may become more disadvantaged than many writers and legal commentators could ever imagine.

Equally important, such a challenge could hold employees liable for damages under copyright infringement when they are required to use the copyrighted materials and have no autonomy or authority to stop the use of the works. Given the problems associated with this potential form of lawsuit, Pulsinelli (2007) advocates protection for public employees through an absolute immunity when public employees use intellectual property works in the context of their employment, regardless of their knowledge. The clear message from the conflict between the sovereign immunity doctrine and provisions of the intellectual property laws over monetary damages is that public colleges and universities may be immune from lawsuits over monetary damages and that creative legal avenues may even hold public employees liable for damages.

Elaborating on the Legal Conundrum

At stake in these cases of public institutions' infringement of another's intellectual property is the ability to collect money derived from the use of the intellectual property (but see Crews and Harper, 1999). The metanarrative underlying these cases, then, is that the modern state is made up of forces that drive its subdivisions to compete with each other and with private entities and that these subdivisions even exceed the interests of the individuals that make them up, as in the *Genentech* case in which the university was at odds with its former professors. The privatization movement in public higher education, therefore, is not merely a reworking of state functions in response to market forces; it is a movement that requires state sanction. From the perspectives of economic, political, and social forces, we have to pay attention to the growth of state governments, the growth and autonomy of their agencies, and the entrepreneurial ideology that drives how they behave, not just because it sheds doubt on their pursuit of public interests but because this activity is sanctioned and protected by law.

While state governments are shifting the burden of funding to individual institutions, decreasing the latter's reliance on the state for revenues and in some cases forcing or encouraging those institutions to privatize themselves, these same institutions wear the mantle of the state to shield them from the law. Increasingly, their budget mechanisms suggest that states are trying to give them even more independence. One may wonder, therefore, whether the idea of sovereign immunity for public institutions of higher education is structurally coherent. Those institutions do tend to separate themselves from state control, often claiming academic freedom against state legislatures. Their history thus makes them odd "arms of the state" in that traditional notions of academic freedom give them a great deal of autonomy.

More fundamentally, these cases shed doubt on the ability of the public to hold their own institutions accountable to it. With public institutions of higher education, the "public good" they serve is one that is also premised on an idea that it is "good of the public" and that they would not harm that public (and if they violate, say, patent rights, they do so "innocently," as the Supreme Court indicated in *College Savings Bank* (1999) and *Florida Prepaid* (1999)). The idea that public colleges and universities are not in business for themselves needs to be dispelled. At the same time, intellectual property holders, particularly of copyrights, may devise a more creative lawsuit to seek damages from parties affiliated with the state, including state employees as individuals who are personally liable. Thus, this conundrum drives states to act freely, privatize, and hold themselves not liable, but the law may not protect state employees from personal liability for actions based on copyright infringement conducted on behalf of the state, nor can the state use its resources to defend its employees sued for personal liability. As Klein (2005) points out, this situation becomes particularly troublesome as online courses increase and professors act more like independent agents, which further substantiates a case for personal liability of a professor at a public institution. Simply put, professors at public institutions may be required to pay for illegal actions of the state while the public colleges and universities behave more like private entities, and both remain responsible for furthering the public good through educational activities.

Chapter Summary

This chapter examined how the laws of patents and copyrights contain shared and related concerns with other areas of law that illustrate treatment of higher education as playing a significant role in commerce and trade, and yet the laws also shield public institutions from trade practices that constitute intellectual property infringement. To uncover these themes of commerce, trade, and public institutions' shield, this chapter addressed trademarks, trade secrets, international treaties pertaining to intellectual property, and state sovereign immunity over infringement.

As the terms signify, trademarks and trade secrets represent activities of trade and commerce. Like patents and copyrights, trademarks and trade secrets serve as additional intellectual property options available to protect the interests of the creator, which in turn fosters more innovation in society as inventors know that their interests may be protected. In higher education, a trademark protects the identity or mark of an entity such as a university, a unit of an organization, or a product or process that an entity developed from unauthorized users. Therefore, the mark reveals to the world the economic and reputational interests that the trademark holder has as applied to the entity, product, or process. Put simply, a trademark attaches an added assurance of keeping the trademark holder's interests contained and blocking unauthorized uses of the trademark so the consuming public does not get confused between two different entities, products, or processes.

In addition, trade secrets protect knowledge by not disclosing valued information. As the critics of trade secrets indicate, this protection fosters organizational hoarding, a practice that is contrary to the norms of the academic environment. At the same time, the protection permits nondisclosure so academic researchers or industry may keep their works free from misappropriation, which in the long run may protect the public from improper handling, use, or exposure to the research findings. Nevertheless, this chapter demonstrated that the legal parameters, technological advancements, and competing interests along with the economic, political, and social forces more broadly shape intellectual property policies and practices at institutions of higher education.

Similarly, the international setting operates heavily off trade principles. In terms of international compliance, international treaties focus on policies that foster foreign markets and access to products and services while also standardizing the concept of protective economic measures without much exception and consideration to the academic environment. The treaties typically establish uniformity among signatory countries in the process and recognition of intellectual property along with basic standards of practice (for example, minimum number of years to recognize a protected work). In the comparative realm, the priorities of trade practices, commercialization of academic works, declining government funding, and other dimensions fit the movement toward academic capitalism.

Although the protections of trademarks and trade secrets and the principles of international law emphasize uniform application of the law, sovereign immunity creates an imbalance in the equal treatment of the law, and it presents a legal conundrum. The state may participate in trade and commerce, and indeed public institutions are expected to do so. At the same time, the state may assert protections over sovereign immunity, which protects state actors from infringement lawsuits.

According to the doctrine of sovereign immunity, state actors cannot be sued without consent, and absent some explicit, affirmative action, states did not waive their sovereign immunity through the enactment of federal intellectual property laws. Consequently, public colleges and universities are immune to lawsuits demanding monetary awards, while private institutions may be sued and held financially liable for the same infringement actions. Viewed another way, the law shifts the balance of power over intellectual property in favor of public institutions. As an alternative for intellectual property holders who seek monetary recovery, the legal literature suggests suing the state employee who initiates the infringement in his or her personal capacity. By pursuing that legal recourse, if the intellectual property holder prevails, the individual state employee must pay from his or her own funds and without the backing of the state. As these matters come to light, the legal parameters, technological advancements, and competing interests will further alter intellectual property policies and practices at colleges and universities.

Conclusion

A S THE INFORMATION AGE emphasizes knowledge, intellectual property escalates as an issue of concern, especially for colleges and universities. Certainly, higher education serves the society of the information age through preparation for the labor force, but equally critical, higher education participates in the commercial world of intellectual property. As an industry that currently transacts with $375 billion in terms of expenditures (Blumenstyk, 2008), higher education no doubt produces, maintains, controls, and trades intellectual property, which requires colleges and universities to construct intellectual property policies and practices balancing several considerations.

In one dimension, intellectual property policies and practices at colleges and universities are shaped by the economic, political, and social forces. The economic forces drive incentives and rewards for creators and holders of intellectual property. The economic value of the intellectual property represents a critical component of national and international policy justifications. Moreover, the economic environment of the information values even more the intangible property. Accordingly, copyright and patent laws protect the interests of the holders through infringement actions, and trademarks and trade secrets protect holders from parties that misappropriate their works.

The political forces advance the power dynamics connected with intellectual property. In copyright law, determinations of fair use, although not binding law, are largely dictated by guidelines established by industry. Similarly, the Recording Industry Association of America and the Motion Picture Association of America garnered sufficient political clout to include provisions in the most recent Higher Education Act's reauthorization to require technological blocks and monitoring of media piracy at U.S. colleges and universities. Patent law also infuses political power with contests over ownership rights between faculty and administrators as well as between the academic community and industry.

The social forces present the relationships and the outcomes. Under the social forces, intellectual property potentially serves the greater good and benefits society by fostering innovation. In copyright and patent laws, writers, artists, publishers, and inventors receive protections, in turn spurring further creative expressions, and society enjoys the products, processes, and expressions that emerge. In addition, the social forces capture more than the consuming public's benefit. Intellectual property contains moral rights such as the rights of attribution and integrity of the products, process, and expressions.

In another dimension, intellectual property policies and practices at colleges and universities are shaped by three factors: legal parameters, technological advancements, and competing interests. The legal parameters include quite obviously intellectual property laws. In addition, as we discussed, contract laws, state laws, international treaties, and even sovereign immunity through the Eleventh Amendment to the U.S. Constitution contribute to policies and practices at institutions of higher education. For example, many institutions of higher education use contract law to grant some financial rewards to university staff who patent their works.

Technological advancements represent a second factor that shapes intellectual property policies and practices at colleges and universities. For example, as discoveries in the biotechnology area developed, higher education and industry sought patents for new subject matter not previously included. Similarly, when subject matter did not qualify for patent protection, institutions of higher education as a matter of policy protected their works as trade secrets. In addition, as technological advancements occurred and made piracy of music and movies easier, colleges and universities proposed alternative, legal downloading avenues and implemented technological applications to curb piracy on campus.

As a third factor, competing interests also shape intellectual property policies and practices at colleges and universities. For instance, as online education emerged as a copyrightable expression, faculty and college administrators vied for a stake in the copyrightable works. Similarly, book publishers established guidelines on fair use to maintain their interests and to influence college and university policies and practices. Under patentable items, we also recognize the competing interests that contributed to intellectual property policies and practices at colleges and universities as members of the academic community desired quality control, access, and rewards.

Our framework attempts to capture the complex economic, political, and social forces that explained the surrounding circumstances. These environmental pressures contributed to the development and refinement of intellectual property policies and practices at colleges and universities along with the legal parameters pertaining to intellectual property, technological advancements that shifted the eligibility and form of intellectual property, and competing interests of various actors who vied for a stake in the intellectual property. Collectively, the factors in the context of the economic, political, and social forces shaped intellectual property policies and practices at colleges and universities.

We focused on the law as illustration of this phenomenon, but attention to other concerns highlights similar issues and similar tensions. We think that the question of whether or not institutions of higher education should play such a role is moot, as the conditions we mentioned have required this participation. Instead, in the field of higher education, this movement, whether inevitable or not, does not go uncontested. Consequently, administrators seeking to engage faculty, researchers, and students more actively in technology transfer and other forms of intellectual property commercialization may be well advised to consider that many faculty, researchers, and students will act unwillingly, which certainly creates tensions in light of the value and emphasis on information.

The reason for tension relates to the beliefs that the university is a public domain and that the privatization of knowledge, which intellectual property laws and policies protect, seems antithetical to this concept of publicness. Some members of the higher education community are sanguine about the forces that will require such privatization and thus try to accommodate the movements toward intellectual property with the ideals of institutions of higher education as public domains. In these cases, the arguments take the form of expanding the concepts of free speech and fair use in copyright law and the research exemption in patent law, limiting the availability of intellectual property rights in certain areas and requiring that universities and other research-oriented entities grant compulsory licenses to their intellectual properties. The most critical argument that institutions should consider is the privatization of knowledge and enclosure of the public domain. These latter critiques require us to ask whether it is appropriate to even own knowledge. We think this central question, while in some ways academic (that is, rhetorical), is nevertheless one with which administrators and others seeking to expand intellectual property policies must contend.

Intellectual property law will shape the course of knowledge for the foreseeable future. This movement does not come without controversy, as the ownership of knowledge severely constrains inter- and intrauniversity relationships. Universities seek greater returns on marketable intellectual property, leading some to question their public role in disseminating knowledge for their own sake and for the sake of the firms. The ownership of knowledge has also dramatically changed the nature of faculty work, so that it becomes redirected from publications to commercially motivated research. Even students begin to see their work as copyrightable. Whether one is in favor of intellectual property or not, no clear understanding of intellectual property law can take place without an understanding of the controversies associated with it that will shape how institutions must behave.

Modern economic analysis now sets the terms for policy discussion. No longer do discussions reflect philosophical questions such as natural rights or just desserts, but in keeping with the utilitarian spirit of the times, the issues relate to whether or not intellectual property enhances economic welfare by stimulating technological progress (David, 1993). On the one hand, economic analysis provides more widely accepted rationales for public intervention, but on the other, it is unable to achieve consensus on the answer to two difficult empirical questions, which it itself has set up: Will faster technological progress always be an unambiguously good thing that warrants the sacrifice of other societal goals? How responsive is the supply of socially useful discoveries and inventions to the creation of greater private economic incentives (David, 1993, pp. 20–21)?

Adding to these broader questions, this monograph presents key issues of intellectual property rights nested in the context of higher education. In particular, it examines the intersection among legal parameters pertaining to intellectual property, technological advancements, and competing interests framed in our information economy and executed under intellectual property law. In doing so, it captures the discussion surrounding the interests, priorities, and influences of multiple actors and the battles for rights among them. Equally important in this framework, the monograph raises significant concerns about how the law and technology can even deal with very practical realities for universities and academic communities. For instance, the law currently requires nonprofit educational institutions to take steps to curb infringement. At what point will new technologies continuously outpace the prior generation's technology so that we can no longer refer to technology change in terms of "generations" but in units of days or minutes? When it occurs, how can universities comply with the laws and stop students, faculty, and staff from infringement? Similarly, the law currently permits use of protected works for limited uses, which are prescribed in ways that make sense today but may not in the future. What is fair use of a digital dissertation? How do academics place limits on use of academic simulations when the simulation is available for an online course? How does the research exemption work with multimedia technology? Likewise, the law prescribes parameters on use of copyrighted works as applied in the United States, but it fails to consider the global environment of education, especially when online education no longer contains the physical divide. If that is the case, how do academic institutions determine the legal parameters? What do universities and members of the academic community do when others do not respect the same intellectual property laws and practices in the United States? How does it change intellectual property law to an international realm not just a nation-state, jurisdictional matter?

We raise these issues because the changes are inevitable and some framework is needed to address these matters. This monograph presented the current state of intellectual property as derived from the law and literature. It trailed the changes in the law and higher education practices and policies, yet we are certain that our discussion will be foreign to scholars in a decade. Indeed, although we cannot forecast what precisely will occur, we suspect that our framework will continue to capture the dimensions (that is, the economic, political, and social forces, which sets the stage for the direct factors of legal parameters, technological advancements, and competing interests that shape intellectual property policies and practices at colleges and universities) that account for these future iterations of intellectual property in the impending, more advanced information age.

Notes

1. At present, few institutions actually make money in technology transfer (Powers, 2006; Thursby and Thursby, 2003); however, as institutions become more efficient through such financial structures (including lowering fixed costs, developing expertise in handling patentable works, and waiting for existing patents to produce more revenue or capital), these technology transfer offices may eventually recognize income to cross-subsidize other parts of the university. Likewise, with the influx of online learning and other technologically mediated creations, we anticipate that many public colleges and universities will begin to recognize new revenue sources from these outlets and that these institutions will likely use these funds to supplement shortfalls from state appropriations and other governmental support.

2. To comply with an international agreement such as the Uruguay Round Trade Agreement, this requirement has one exception. Unauthorized sound recordings of live performances, which are not fixed in any tangible medium of expression, also violate a provision in the copyright act (17 U.S.C. §1101).

3. Robinson (2000) notes that courts determine the stature qualification based on "opinions of artists, art dealers, collectors of fine art, curators of art museums, restorers and conservators of fine art, and other persons involved with the creation, appreciation, history, or marketing of fine art" (p. 1945).

4. In addition to the legal issues over copyright ownership of faculty scholarship, Springer (2005) identified two very practical matters as to why

colleges typically do not assert any ownership over these works. "If the administration owned all the work of faculty, then it would be responsible for the content. Few administrations want to claim responsibility for every conclusion reached by faculty." In addition, "if the institution owned the scholarly work of faculty, it would also be responsible for things like negotiating book contracts, publishing agreements, handling revisions and updates, etc. Few institutions have the desire or resources to take this on" (http://www.aaup.org/NR/exeres/517C85B6-CC13-4A47-AE3E-5C1763713B02.htm).

5. The Court raised the issue by stating, "In determining whether a hired party is an employee under the general common law of agency, we consider the hiring party's right to control the manner and means by which the product is accomplished" (p. 751).

6. The trade associations that have participated in the peer-to-peer copyright infringement dialogue include American Society of Media Photographers, Association of American Publishers, Association of American University Presses, Authors Guild, Inc., Business Software Alliance, Directors Guild of America, Entertainment Software Alliance, Independent Film & Television Alliance, Motion Picture Association of American, National Music Photographers of America, Professional Photographers of America, Recording Industry Association of America, Screen Actors Guild, and Software and Information Industry Association.

7. According to the report, the calculation is "based primarily on a review of confidential sources" (Siwek, 2007, p. 7). Although the calculation of the downloads is not disclosed, the number is plausible in light of the other reports (see, for example, Kruger, 2004).

8. See, for example, *Fenn v. Yale University* (2003); *Kucharczyk v. the Regents of the University of California* (1996); *University of West Virginia Board of Trustees v. Vanvoorhies* (2002).

9. Semiconductor chips pose similar dilemmas, as they are expensive to make but easy to reproduce. Furthermore, the chips are too functional for copyright protection, but their technology is fairly well known now and so they do not qualify as novelties or nonobvious inventions. Thus, the United

States decided on a special protection and in 1984 passed the Semiconductor Chip Protection Act, which borrows from existing copyright and patent law but offers only ten years of protection (Wallerstein, Mogee, and Schoen, 1993).

10. University-Industry Partnership is a consortium of several organizational representatives with a charge to facilitate contracts between universities and industry.

11. A patent infringement action occurs after a patent issuance against an opposing party that is claimed to have no rights to the patent or license to the patent. In contrast, an interference proceeding typically refers to challenges made during the initiating party's patent application.

12. Trade names are typically subsumed into the intellectual property category of trademarks.

13. See *College Savings Bank* v. *Florida Prepaid Postsecondary Education Expense Board* (1999) and *Florida Prepaid Postsecondary Education Expense Board* v. *College Savings Bank* (1999); these cases applied the sovereign immunity doctrine to patent law. See also *Seminole Tribe* v. *Florida* (1996).

14. The Takings Clause is the basis for a public entity's payments when it takes property under authority of eminent domain.

References

Ahrens, F. (2003, April 4). Four students sued over music sites: Industry group targets file sharing at colleges. *Washington Post,* p. E1.

Altbach, P. G., Berdahl, R. O., and Gumport, P. J. (2005). American higher education in the twenty-first century: Social, political, and economic challenges (2nd ed.). Baltimore: Johns Hopkins University Press.

Aoki, K. (1998). The stakes of intellectual property law. In D. Kairys (Ed.), *The politics of law: A progressive critique* (3rd ed., pp. 259–278). New York: Basic Books.

Apple, R. D. (1989). Patenting university research: Harry Steenbock and the Wisconsin Alumni Research Foundation. *Isis,* 80(3), 375–394.

Apple, R. D. (1996). *Vitamania: Vitamins in American culture.* New Brunswick, NJ: Rutgers University Press.

Arewa, O. B. (2006). From J.C. Bach to hip hop: Musical borrowing, copyright, and cultural context. *North Carolina Law Review,* 84(2), 547–645.

Aronauer, R. (2005). Separated at birth. *Chronicle of Higher Education,* 52(11), A9.

Ashley, C. L. (2004). The TEACH Act: Higher education challenges for compliance. *ECAR Research Bulletin,* 2004(13), 1–11.

Association of University Technology Managers (2005). *AUTM licensing survey: FY 2004 survey summary,* Northbrook, IL: Author.

Association of University Technology Managers (2007). *AUTM licensing survey: FY 2006 survey summary,* Northbrook, IL: Author.

Audette, L. G. (1980). A model rights and ownership of educational materials policy for institutions. *Journal of Biocommunication,* 7(1), 4–10.

Autry, J. R. (2002). Toward a definition of striking similarity in infringement actions for copyrighted musical works. *Journal of Intellectual Property Law,* 10(1), 113–141.

Baez, B. (2005). Private knowledge, public domain: The politics of intellectual property in higher education. In D. R. Boyles (Ed.), *Schools or markets? Commercialization, privatization, and school-business partnerships* (pp. 119–148). Mahwah, NJ: Lawrence Erlbaum Associates.

Baez, B., and Slaughter, S. (2001). Academic freedom and federal courts in the 1990s: The legitimation of the conservative entrepreneurial state. In J. Smart and W. G. Tierney

(Eds.), *Higher education: Handbook of theory and research* (Vol. 16, pp. 73–118). Edison, NJ: Agathon Press.

Bagley, M. A. (2006). Academic discourse and proprietary rights: Putting patents in their proper place. *Boston College Law Review, 47,* 217–274.

Barnett, A. T. (2001). "Profiting at my expense": An analysis of the commercialization of professors' lecture notes. *Journal of Intellectual Property Law, 9,* 137–162.

Barton, J. H. (1993). Adapting the intellectual property system to new technologies. In M. B. Wallerstein, M. E. Mogee, and R. A. Schoen (Eds.), *Global dimensions of intellectual property rights in science and technology,* pp. 256–283. Washington, DC: National Academy Press.

Bartow, A. (1998). Educational fair use in copyright: Reclaiming the right to photocopy freely. *University of Pittsburgh Law Review, 60,* 149–230.

Bearby, S., and Siegal, B. (2002). From the stadium parking lot to the information superhighway: How to protect your trademark from infringement. *Journal of College and University Law, 28,* 633–662.

Benjamin, R. (2003). The environment of American higher education: A constellation of changes. *Annals of the American Academy of Political and Social Science, 585,* 8–30.

Berneman, L. (2003). University-industry collaborations: Partners in research promoting productivity and economic growth. *Research Management Review, 13,* 1–10.

Bhattacharjee, S., Gopal, R. D., and Sanders, G. L. (2003). Digital music and online sharing: Software piracy 2.0? *Communications of the ACM, 46*(7), 107–111.

Blue Coat Systems. (2004). *Establishing an Internet use policy to address peer-to-peer (P2P) use.* Sunnyvale, CA: Blue Coat Systems.

Blumenstyk, G. (1991, February 6). U. of N.C. must disclose some data on animal research. *Chronicle of Higher Education, 37*(21), A26.

Blumenstyk, G. (1994, September 7). Trade-secret dispute. *Chronicle of Higher Education, 41*(2), A5.

Blumenstyk, G. (1995, April 14). Wayne State U. to surrender key patent rights to company. *Chronicle of Higher Education, 41*(31), A36.

Blumenstyk, G. (1998, January 23). "Virtual classroom" is a trademark of New Jersey Institute of Technology. *Chronicle of Higher Education, 44*(20), A25.

Blumenstyk, G. (2004, April 30). U. of Colorado to collect, finally, $58-million drug-patent judgment. *Chronicle of Higher Education, 50*(34), A28.

Blumenstyk, G. (2005, October 14). Federal appeals court upholds denial of DNA patent. *Chronicle of Higher Education, 52*(8), A26.

Blumenstyk, G. (2008, October 3). The $375-billion question: Why does college cost so much? *Chronicle of Higher Education, 55*(6), A1.

Blumenthal, D., and others. (1986). University-industry research relationships in biotechnology: Implications for the university. *Science, 232*(4756), 1361–1366.

Blumenthal, D., Campbell, E. G., Causino, N., and Louis, K. S. (1996). Participation of life-science faculty in research relationships with industry. *New England Journal of Medicine, 335*(23), 1734–1739.

Blumenthal, D., Causino, N., Campbell, E. G., and Louis, K. S. (1996). Relationships between academic institutions and industry in the life sciences: An industry survey. *New England Journal of Medicine, 334*(6), 368–373.

Bobbitt, W. R. (2006). *Universities, faculty, and the battle over intellectual property: Who owns what's inside the professor's head?* Lewiston, NY: Edwin Mellen Press.

Boettiger, S., and Bennett, A. B. (2006). Bayh-Dole: If we knew then what we know now. *Nature Biotechnology, 24*(3), 320–323.

Borow, T. A. (1998). Copyright ownership of scholarly works created by university faculty and posted on school-provided Web pages. *University of Miami Business Law Review, 7,* 149–169.

Bowers, L. J., and Leon, V. (1994). Patent policies of 65 educational institutions: A comparison. *SRA Journal, 25*(4), 5–12.

Boyle, J. (1997). A politics of intellectual property: Environmentalism for the net? *Duke Law Journal, 47,* 87–116.

Brown, M. T., Zuefle, D. M., and Batista, P. J. (2007). Will the real 12th man please stand up?: Texas A&M and Seattle Seahawks settle dispute over right to identify fans as "12th Man". *Sport Marketing Quarterly, 16*(2), 115–117.

Bush, V. (1945). *Science: The endless frontier.* Washington, DC: U.S. Government Printing Office.

Campbell, E. G., Louis, K. S., and Blumenthal, D. (1998). Looking a gift horse in the mouth: Corporate gifts supporting life sciences research. *Journal of the American Medical Association, 279*(13), 995–999.

Campbell, E. G., and others. (2002). Data withholding in academic genetics: Evidence from a national survey. *Journal of the American Medical Association, 287*(4), 473–480.

Campbell, E. G., Powers, J. B., Blumenthal, D., and Biles, B. (2004). Inside the triple helix: Technology transfer and commercialization in the life sciences. *Health Affairs, 23*(1), 64–76.

Campbell, E. G., Weissman, J. S., Causino, N., and Blumenthal, D. (2000). Academic medicine: Characteristics of faculty denied access to research results and biomaterials. *Research Policy, 29*(2), 303–312.

Campbell, T.I.D., and Slaughter, S. (1999). Faculty and administrators' attitudes toward potential conflicts of interest, commitment, and equity in university-industry relationships. *Journal of Higher Education, 70*(3), 309–352.

Carlson, S. (2002, April 26). Phynd finds a niche. *Chronicle of Higher Education,* p. A36.

Carlson, S. (2003, May 23). A victim of file sharing. *Chronicle of Higher Education,* p. A28.

Carnevale, D., and Young, J. R. (1999, December 17). Who owns online courses? Colleges and professors start to sort it out. *Chronicle of Higher Education,* p. A45.

Carroll, M. W. (2007). Fixing fair use. *North Carolina Law Review, 85*(4), 1087–1154.

Casey, J. J., Jr. (2004). Developing harmonious university-industry partnerships. *University of Dayton Law Review, 30,* 245–263.

Castagnera, J. O., Fine, C. R., and Belfiore, A. (2002). Protecting intellectual capital in the new century: Are universities prepared? *Duke Law & Technology Review, 2002*(10), 1–10.

Chew, P. K. (1992). Faculty-generated inventions: Who owns the golden egg? *Wisconsin Law Review*, 1992, 259–314.

Chmielewski, D. C. (2003, May 2). Students settle in lawsuit over file swapping. *San Jose Mercury News*, 1E.

Clarkson, G., and DeKorte, D. (2006). The problem of patent thickets in convergent technologies. *Annals of the New York Academy of Sciences, 1093*, 180–200.

Cohen, W. M., and Walsh, J. P. (2007). Real impediments to academic biomedical research. In A. B. Jaffe, J. Lerner, and S. Stern (Eds.), *Innovation policy and the economy* (Vol. 8, National Bureau of Economic Research Innovation Policy and the Economy). Chicago: University of Chicago Press Journals.

Crews, K. D. (1993). *Copyright, fair use, and the challenge for universities: Promoting the progress of higher education.* Chicago: University of Chicago Press.

Crews, K. D. (2001). The law of fair use and the illusion of fair-use guidelines. *Ohio State Law Journal, 62*(2), 602–700.

Crews, K. D. (2002). *New copyright law for distance education: The meaning and importance of the TEACH Act.* Retrieved October 20, 2007, from http://www.copyright.iupui.edu/teach_summary.htm.

Crews, K. D., and Harper, G. K. (1999). The immunity dilemma: Are state colleges and universities still liable for copyright infringements? *Journal of the American Society for Information Science, 50*(14), 1350–1352.

Dai, Y., Popp, D., and Bretschneider, S. (2005). Institutions and intellectual property: The influence of institutional forces on university patenting. *Journal of Policy Analysis and Management, 24*(3), 579–598.

Daniel, P.T.K., and Pauken, P. D. (1999). The impact of the electronic media on instructor creativity and institutional ownership within copyright law. *Education Law Reporter, 132*, 1–20.

David, P. A. (1993). Intellectual property institutions and the panda's thumb: Patents, copyrights, and trade secrets in economic theory and history. In M. B. Wallerstein, M. E. Mogee, and R. A. Schoen (Eds.), *Global dimensions of intellectual property rights in science and technology* (pp. 19–61). Washington, DC: National Academy Press.

de Larena, L. R. (2007). The price of progress: Are universities adding to the cost? *Houston Law Review, 43*(5), 1373–1444.

Demaine, L. J., and Fellmeth, A. X. (2002). Reinventing the double helix: A novel and nonobvious reconceptualization of the biotechnology patent. *Stanford Law Review, 55*(2), 303–462.

Denicola, R. C. (2006). Copyright and open access: Reconsidering university ownership of faculty research. *Nebraska Law Review, 85,* 351–382.

Dillen, J. S. (1997). DNA patentability: Anything but obvious. *Wisconsin Law Review*, 1997, 1023–1046.

Dinwoodie, G. B., and Okediji, R. L. (2004). The international intellectual property law system: New actors, new institutions, new sources. *American Society of International Law*, 213–222.

Doellinger, C. J. (2007). A new theory of trademarks. *Penn State Law Review, 111,* 823–861.

Drechsler, C. T. (2008). Annotation: Application and effect of "shop right rule" or license giving employer limited rights in employees' inventions and discoveries. *American Law Reports 2d, 61,* 356–448.

Dreyfuss, R. C. (1987). The creative employee and the Copyright Act of 1976. *University of Chicago Law Review, 54*(2), 590–647.

Dutton, W. (Ed.). (2002). *Digital academe.* New York: Routledge.

Ebenstein, D. (1987). Copyright infringement litigation and fair use. *Practising Law Institute Introduction to Copyright and Trademark Law, 238,* 151–256.

Eisenberg, R. S. (1996). Public research and private development: patents and technology transfer in government-sponsored research. *Virginia Law Review, 82*(8), 1663–1727.

Eisenberg, R. S. (2003). Patent swords and shields. *Science, 299*(5609), 1018–1019.

Electronic Frontier Foundation. (2007). *RIAA v. the people: Four years later.* San Francisco: Electronic Frontier Foundation.

Etzkowitz, H., Webster, A., Gebhardt, C., and Terra, B.R.C. (2000). The future of the university and the university of the future: Evolution of ivory tower to entrepreneurial paradigm. *Research Policy, 29*(2), 313–330.

Ficsor, M. (2006). The WIPO "internet treaties:" The United States as the driver: The United States as the main source of obstruction—as seen by an antirevolutionary central European. *John Marshall Review of Intellectual Property Law, 6*(1), 17–39.

Fine, C. R., and Castagnera, J. O. (2003). Should there be a corporate concern? Examining American university intellectual property policies. *Journal of Intellectual Capital, 4*(1), 49–60.

Fisher, W. W., III. (1988). Reconstructing the fair use doctrine. *Harvard Law Review, 101*(8), 1659–1795.

Frazier, K. (1999). What's wrong with fair-use guidelines for the academic community? *Journal of the American Society for Information Science, 50*(14), 1320–1323.

Frost, G. E. (1967). The 1967 patent law debate: First-to-invent vs. first-to-file. *Duke Law Journal, 1967*(5), 923–942.

Garabedian, T. E. (2002). Nontraditional publications and their effect on patentable inventions. *Nature Biotechnology, 20,* 401–402.

Gasaway, L. N. (2001a). Balancing copyright concerns: The TEACH Act of 2001. *EDUCAUSE Review, 36*(6), 82–83.

Gasaway, L. N. (2001b). Impasse: The impact of technological change on the creation, dissemination, and protection of intellectual property. *Ohio State Law Journal, 62*(2), 783–820.

Geiger, R. L. (1986). *To advance knowledge: The growth of American research universities, 1900–1940.* New York: Oxford University Press.

Geiger, R. L. (1993). *Research and relevant knowledge: American research universities since World War II.* New York: Oxford University Press.

Geiger, R. L. (2004). *Knowledge and money: Research universities and the paradox of the marketplace.* Stanford, CA: Stanford University Press.

Gross, M. (2005). *Higher education unlicensed software experience: Student and academics survey.* Washington, DC: Business Software Alliance.

Gulbrandsen, C. E. (2007). Bayh-Dole: Wisconsin roots and inspired public policy. *Wisconsin Law Review, 2007*(6), 1149–1163.

Hall, B. H., Link, A. N., and Scott, J. T. (2003). Universities as research partners. *Review of Economics and Statistics, 85*(2), 485–491.

Hammersla, A. M. (2006). *A primer on intellectual property.* Washington, DC: National Council of University Research Administrators.

Harmon, A. (2003, April 23). Recording industry goes after students over music sharing. *New York Times,* A1.

Heathington, K. W., Heathington, B. S., & Roberson, A. J. (1986). Commercializing intellectual properties at major research universities: Income distribution. *Society of Research Administration Journal, 17*(4), 27–38.

Heller, M. A., and Eisenberg, R. S. (1998). Can patents deter innovation? The anticommons in biomedical research. *Science 280*(5364), 698–701.

Henderson, R., Jaffe, A. J., and Trajtenberg, M. (1998). Universities as a source of commercial technology: A detailed analysis of university patenting, 1965–1988. *Review of Economics and Statistics, 80*(1), 119–127.

Hermanowicz, J. C. (1998). *The stars are not enough: Scientists—their passions and professions.* Chicago: University of Chicago Press.

Hettinger, E. C. (1989). Justifying intellectual property. *Philosophy and Public Affairs, 18,* 31–52.

Hirtle, P. B. (2008). *Copyright term and the public domain in the United States.* Ithaca, NY: Cornell Copyright Information Center. Retrieved February 8, 2008, from http://www.copyright.cornell.edu/public_domain/copyrightterm.pdf.

Hobbs, R., Jaszi, P., and Aufderheide, P. (2007). *The cost of copyright confusion for media literacy.* Washington, DC: Center for Social Media, American University.

Holman, C. M. (2007). Is Lilly written description a paper tiger? A comprehensive assessment of the impact of Eli Lilly and its progeny in the courts and PTO. *Albany Law Journal of Science and Technology, 17,* 1–85.

Holmes, G., and Levin, D. A. (2000). Who owns course materials prepared by a teacher or professor? The application of copyright law to teaching materials in the internet age. *Brigham Young University Education and Law Journal, 2000,* 165–189.

Huber, J., Yeh, B. T., and Jeweler, R. (2006). *Copyright exemptions for distance education: 17 U.S.C. §110(2), the Technology, Education, and Copyright Harmonization Act of 2002.* Washington, DC: Congressional Research Service.

Intellectual Property Institute (2006). *File-sharing survey.* Richmond, VA: National CyberEducation Project, University of Richmond School of Law. Retrieved January 25, 2008, from http://www.law.richmond.edu/ipi/pdf/SurveyResults.pdf.

Jobe, J. (2006). Colleges, code, and copyright: The impact of digital networks and technological controls on copyright and the dissemination of information in higher education. *College & Research Libraries, 67*(3), 278–281.

Johnson, C. (2006). Degrees of deception: Are consumers and employers being duped by online universities and diploma mills? *Journal of College and University Law, 32,* 411–490.

Jones, S. (2002). *The Internet goes to college.* Washington, DC: Pew Internet & American Life Project.

Kaplin, W. A., and Lee, B. A. (2006). *The law of higher education.* San Francisco: Jossey-Bass.

Katz, R. N. (1998). *Dancing with the devil: Information technology and the new competition in higher education.* San Francisco: Jossey-Bass.

Kehoe, B. T. (2005). The TEACH Act's eligibility requirements: Good policy of a bad compromise? *Brooklyn Law Review, 71*(2), 1029–1063.

Kelley, K. B., Bonner, K., McMichael, J. S., and Pomea, N. (2002). Intellectual property, ownership and digital course materials: A study of intellectual property policies at two and four year colleges and universities. *portal: Libraries and the Academy, 2*(2), 255–266.

Kesselheim, A. S., and Avorn, J. (2005). University-based science and biotechnology products: Defining the boundaries of intellectual property. *Journal of the American Medical Association, 293*(7), 850–854.

Keyser, M. W. (2005). The academic mission and copyright law: Are these values in conflict? In Center for Intellectual Property, University of Maryland University College: *Colleges, code, and copyright: The impact of digital networks and technological controls on copyright and the dissemination of information in higher education.* Chicago: Association of College and Research Libraries.

Kilby, P. A. (1995). The discouragement of learning: Scholarship made for hire. *Journal of College and University Law, 21*(3), 455–488.

Klein, M. W. (2004). "The equitable rule": Copyright ownership of distance-education courses. *Journal of College and University Law, 31,* 143–192.

Klein, M. W. (2005). "Sovereignty of reason": An approach to sovereign immunity and copyright ownership of distance-education courses at public colleges and universities. *Journal of Law and Education, 34,* 199–254.

Korn, D. E. (1987). Patent and trade secret protection in university-industry research relationships in biotechnology. *Harvard Journal on Legislation, 24*(1), 191–238.

Kruger, B. (2004). Failing intellectual property protection 101. *T.H.E. Journal, 31*(9), 48.

Kulkarni, S. R. (1995). All professors create equally: Why faculty should have complete control over the intellectual property rights in their creations. *Hastings Law Journal, 47,* 221–256.

Kwall, R. R. (2001). Copyright issues in online courses: Ownership, authorship and conflict. *Santa Clara Computer and High Technology Law Journal, 18,* 1–34.

Landes, W. M., and Posner, R. A. (2003). *Economic structure of intellectual property law.* Cambridge, MA: Belknap.

Lane, J. E., and Healy, M. A. (2005). File sharing, Napster, and institutional responses: Educative, developmental, or responsive policy? *NASPA Journal, 42*(4), 534–548.

Lane, J. E., and Hendrickson, R. M. (2005). Digital copyrights and student file sharing: Educational responsibilities and legal liability for schools, colleges, and universities. *West's Educational Law Reporter, 199,* 19–25.

Lape, L. G. (1992). Ownership of copyrightable works of university professors: The interplay between the copyright act and university copyright policies. *Villanova Law Review, 37,* 223–269.

Lattinville, R. (1996). Logo cops: The law and business of collegiate licensing. *Kansas Journal of Law and Public Policy, 5*(3), 81–124.

Laughlin, G. K. (2000). Who owns the copyright to faculty-created Web sites? The work-for-hire doctrine's applicability to Internet resources created for distance learning and traditional classroom courses. *Boston College Law Review, 41,* 549.

Leaffer, M. A. (1998). The new world of international trademark law. *Marquette Intellectual Property Review, 2,* 1–31.

Lederman, D. (2006, July 10). $25M for U. of Ala. in patent suit. *Inside Higher Education.* Retrieved December 14, 2007, from http://www.insidehighered.com/news/2006/07/10/qt.

Lehman, B. A. (1998). *The Conference on Fair Use: Final report to the commissioner on the conclusion of the Conference on Fair Use.* Washington, DC: U.S. Patent and Trademark Office.

Lenhart, A., and Fox, S. (2000). *Downloading free music: Internet music lovers don't think it's stealing.* Washington, DC: Pew Internet & American Life Project.

Levine, A. E., and Sun, J. C. (2003). *Barriers to distance education: Governmental, legal, and institutional.* Washington, DC: American Council on Education.

Lieberwitz, R. L. (2003). University science research funding: Privatizing policy and practice. In R. G. Ehrenberg and P. E. Stephan (Eds.), *Science and the University.* Ithaca, NY: Cornell Higher Education Research Institute.

Lieberwitz, R. L. (2005). Confronting the privatization and commercialization of academic research: An analysis of social implications at the local, national, and global levels. *Indiana Journal of Global Legal Studies, 12*(1), 109–152.

Liebowitz, S. (2002). *Policing pirates in the networked age.* Washington, DC: Cato Institute.

Lipinski, T. A. (2003). The climate of distance education in the 21st century: Understanding and surviving the changes brought by the TEACH (Technology, Education, and Copyright Harmonization) Act of 2002. *Journal of Academic Librarianship, 29*(6), 362–374.

Litman, J. (1990). The public domain. *Emory Law Journal, 39,* 965–1023.

Loggie, K. A., Barron, A. E., Gulitz, E., Hohlfeld, T., Kromrey, J. D., and Sweeney, P. C. (2007). Intellectual property and online courses: Policies at major research universities. *Quarterly Review of Distance Education, 8*(2), 109–126.

Loggie, K. A., Barron, A. E., Gulitz, E., Hohlfeld, T., Kromrey, J. D., Venable, M., and Sweeney, P. C. (2006). An analysis of copyright policies for distance learning materials at major research universities. *Journal of Interactive On-line Learning, 5*(3), 224–242.

Madden, M., and Lenhart, A. (2003). *Music downloading, file-sharing and copyright.* Washington, DC: Pew Internet & American Life Project.

Madden, M., and Rainie, L. (2005). *Music and video downloading moves beyond P2P.* Washington, DC: Pew Internet & American Life Project.

Manas, A. E. (2003). Harvard as a model in trademark and domain name protection. *Rutgers Computer & Technology Law Journal, 29,* 475–502.

Maxwell, B., Turley, P., Warren, J., and Wright, N. J. (2003). Overview of licensing technology from universities. In *Practising Law Institute, Patents, copyrights, trademarks, and literary property course handbook series* (pp. 507–582). New York: Author.

May, C. (2000). *A global political economy of intellectual-property rights: The new enclosures?* New York: Routledge.

McIsaac, M. S., and Rowe, J. (1997). Ownership and access: Copyright and intellectual property in the on-line environment. In C. L. Dillon and R. Cintrón, *Legal issues in the community college (New Directions for Community Colleges, No. 99)* (pp. 83–92). San Francisco, CA: Jossey-Bass, Inc.

McSherry, C. (2001). *Who owns academic work? Battling for control of intellectual property.* Cambridge, MA: Harvard University Press.

Mello, M. M., Clarridge, B. R., and Studdert, D. M. (2005). Academic medical centers' standards for clinical-trial agreements with industry. *New England Journal of Medicine, 352*(21), 2202–2210.

Mendoza, P., and Berger, J. B. (2005). Patenting productivity and intellectual property policies at research I universities: An exploratory comparative study. *Education Policy Analysis Archives, 13*(5), 1–20.

Merges, R., and Nelson, R. (1990). On the complex economics of patent scope. *Columbia Law Review, 90,* 839–916.

Merges, R., and Nelson, R. (1994). On limiting or encouraging rivalry in technical progress: The effect of patent scope decisions. *Journal of Economic Behavior and Organization, 25*(1), 1–24.

Merton R. K., (1968). *Social theory and social structure.* New York: Free Press.

Merton R. K., (1973). *The sociology of science: Theoretical and empirical investigations.* Chicago: University of Chicago Press.

Metcalfe, A., Diaz, V., and Wagoner, R. (2003). Academic, technology, society, and the market: Four frames of reference for copyright and fair use. *portal: Libraries and the Academy, 3*(2), 191–206.

Metlay, G. (2006). Reconsidering renormalization: Stability and change in 20th-century views on university patents. *Social Studies of Science, 36*(4), 565–597.

Meyer, M. L. (1998). To promote the progress of science and useful arts: The protection of and rights in scientific research. *IDEA: The Journal of Law and Technology, 39,* 1–34.

Miyoshi, M. (2000). Ivory tower in escrow. *boundary 2, 27*(1), 7–50.

Monaghan, P. (2006). Digital dissertation dust-up. *Chronicle of Higher Education, 52*(34), A41.

Moore, R., and McMullan, E. C. (2004). Perceptions of peer-to-peer file sharing among university students. *Journal of Criminal Justice and Popular Culture, 11*(1), 1–19.

Mowery, D. C., Nelson, R. R., Sampat, B. N., and Ziedonis, A. A. (2001). The growth of patenting and licensing by U.S. universities: An assessment of the effects of the Bayh-Dole Act of 1980. *Research Policy, 30*(1), 99–119.

Mowery, D. C., and Sampat, B. N. (2001a). Patenting and licensing university inventions: Lessons from the history of research corporation. *Industrial and Corporate Change, 10*(2), 317–355.

Mowery, D. C., and Sampat, B. N. (2001b). University patents and patent policy debates in the USA, 1925–1980. *Industrial and Corporate Change, 10*(3), 781–814.

Mowery, D. C., and Ziedonis, A. A. (2002). Academic patent quality and quantity before and after the Bayh-Dole Act in the United States. *Research Policy, 31*(3), 399–418.

Munzer, S. R. (1990). *A theory of property.* London: Cambridge University Press.

Myers, P. E. (2003). Developing an intellectual property policy at a predominantly undergraduate institution. *Journal of Research Administration, 34*(1), 8–13.

National Association of College and University Business Officers. (1978). *Patent and copyright policies at selected universities.* Washington, DC: National Association of College and University Business Officers.

National Science Board (1993). *Science and engineering indicators: 1993.* Washington, DC: National Science Foundation.

Nelson, R. R. (2001). Observations on the post–Bayh-Dole rise of patenting at American universities. *Journal of Technology Transfer, 26*(1/2), 13–19.

Nelson, R. R. (2002). The simple economics of basic scientific research. In P. Mirowski (Ed.), *Science bought and sold: Essays in the economics of science* (pp. 151–164). Chicago: University of Chicago Press.

Newberg, J. A., and Dunn, R. L. (2002). Keeping secrets in the campus lab: Law, values and rules of engagement for industry-university R&D partnerships. *American Business Law Journal, 39,* 187–240.

Oberholzer-Gee, F., and Strumpf, K. (2007). The effect of file sharing on record sales: An empirical analysis. *Journal of Political Economy, 115*(1), 1–42.

O'Connor, K. W. (1991). Patenting animals and other living things. *Southern California Law Review, 65,* 597–621.

O'Donnell, M. L., and Parker, C. W. (2005, May 27). How colleges can navigate the thicket of federal regulations. *Chronicle of Higher Education,* p. B5.

"Ohio U. and Ohio State U. settle trademark tussle over 'Ohio.'" *Chronicle of Higher Education, 45*(42), A47.

Okediji, R. (2003). Public welfare and the role of the WTO: Reconsidering the TRIPS agreement. *Emory International Law Review, 17,* 819–918.

Ostergard, R. L. (1998). Intellectual property: A universal human right? *Human Rights Quarterly, 21,* 156–178.

Packard, A. (2002). Copyright or copy wrong: An analysis of university claims to faculty work. *Communication Law and Policy, 7,* 275–315.

Palaima, T. G. (2006, November 17). The real price of college sports. *Chronicle of Higher Education, 53*(13), B12.

Palmer, A. M. (1934). University patent policies. *Journal of the Patent Office Society, 16,* 2.

Patel, S. H. (1996). Graduate students' ownership and attribution rights in intellectual property. *Indiana Law Journal, 71,* 481–512.

Phillips, M. (2007, January 18). Logos mean more than ever. *Knight Ridder Tribune Business News (Washington)*, 1.

"Piracy on University Networks: Hearing Before the Subcommittee on Courts, the Internet, and Intellectual Property House Comm. on the Judiciary," 110th Congress, 1st Session (March 8, 2007) (statement of Jim Davis, Associate Vice Chancellor, University of California), reprinted in Federal Document Clearing House, available on Westlaw at 2007 WL 690300.

Powell, W. W., and Owen-Smith, J. (1998). Universities and the market for intellectual property in the life sciences. *Journal of Policy Analysis and Management, 17*(2), 253–277.

Powers, J. B. (2006). Between lab bench and marketplace: The pitfalls of technology transfer. *Chronicle of Higher Education, 53*(5), B18.

Press, E., and Washburn, J. (2000). The kept university. *Atlantic Monthly, 285*(3), 39–54.

"Pressing legal issues: 10 views of the next 5 years." (2004). *Chronicle of Higher Education, 50*(42), B4.

Pressman, L., and others. (2006). The licensing of DNA patents by US academic institutions: An empirical survey. *Nature Biotechnology, 24*(1), 31–39.

Price, D. K. (1954). *Government and science: Their dynamic relation in American democracy.* New York: New York University Press.

"Princeton settles suit over a former name." (1996, September 20). Retrieved May 6, 2006, from http://query.nytimes.com/gst/fullpage.html?res=9801E4DF143DF933A1575AC0A960958260.

Pulsinelli, G. (2006). Share and share alike: Increasing access to government-funded inventions under the Bayh-Dole Act. *Minnesota Journal of Law, Science & Technology, 7*(2), 393–482.

Pulsinelli, G. (2007). Freedom to explore: Using the Eleventh Amendment to liberate researchers at state universities from liability for intellectual property infringements. *Washington Law Review, 82*(2), 275–376.

Pusser, B. (2004). *Burning down the house: Politics, governance, and affirmative action at the University of California.* Albany, NY: State University of New York Press.

Rai, A. K. (1999). Regulating scientific research: Intellectual property rights and the norms of science. *Northwestern Law Review, 94*(1), 77–152.

Ramirez, H. H. (2004). Defending the privatization of research tools: An examination of the "tragedy of the anticommons" in biotechnology research and development. *Emory Law Journal, 53*(1), 359–389.

Read, B. (2005a, January 14). Coming soon to a campus near you: Movie-industry lawsuits. *Chronicle of Higher Education*, p. A31.

Read, B. (2005b, January 28). Is there a pattern to the music industry's file-sharing lawsuits? *Chronicle of Higher Education*, p. A39.

Read, B. (2006a, April 28). Entertainment industries ask colleges to monitor local networks for piracy. *Chronicle of Higher Education*, p. A39.

Read, B. (2006b, February 3). Students say peer-to-peer service drove them to piracy. *Chronicle of Higher Education*, p. A37.

Read, B. (2007, April 13). Students take cinematic license. *Chronicle of Higher Education*, p. A39.

"Reducing Peer-to-Peer (P2P) Piracy on University Campuses: A Progress Update Hearing Before the Subcommittee on Courts, the Internet, and Intellectual Property House

Comm. on the Judiciary," 109th Congress, 1st Session (September 22, 2005) (statement of Daniel A. Updegrove, Vice President for Information Technology, University of Texas at Austin), reprinted in Federal Document Clearing House, available on Westlaw at 2005 WL 2319084.

Reimertshofer, J. F. (1997). Trademark protection of intercollegiate names, logos, colors and trade dress: A comparison between the United States and Germany. *New York International Law Review, 10,* 131–175.

Rhoades, G. (1998). *Managed professionals: Unionized faculty and restructuring academic labor.* Albany: State University of New York Press.

Rhoades, G., and Slaughter, S. (1991). Professors, administrators, and patents: The negotiation of technology transfer. *Sociology of Education, 64*(2), 65–77.

Rife, M. C., and Hart-Davidson, W. (2006). *Is there a chilling of digital communication? Exploring how knowledge and understanding of the fair use doctrine may influence Web composing.* Social Science Research Network. Retrieved December 10, 2007, from http://ssrn.com/abstract=918822.

Rob, R., and Waldfogel, J. (2006). Piracy on the high C's: Music downloading, sales displacement, and social welfare in a sample of college students. *Journal of Law and Economics, 49*(1), 29–62.

Robbins, J. (2006). Shaping patent policy: The National Research Council and the universities from World War I to the 1960s. In R. Geiger (Ed.), *Perspectives on the History of Higher Education: 2006* (Vol. 25, pp. 89–122). New Brunswick, NJ: Transaction Publishers.

Robinson, C. J. (2000). The "recognized stature" standard in the Visual Artists Rights Act. *Fordham Law Review, 68*(5), 1935–1976.

Rothman, J. E. (2007). The questionable use of custom in intellectual property. *Virginia Law Review, 93*(8), 1899–1982.

Salomon, K. D. (1999). *Copyright consideration in distance education and technology-mediated instruction.* Washington, DC: American Association of Community Colleges.

Sampat, B. N., Mowery, D. C., and Ziedonis, A. A. (2003). Changes in university patent quality after the Bayh–Dole act: A re-examination. *International Journal of Industrial Organization, 21,* 1371–1390.

Samuelson, P. (1993). A case study on computer programs. In M. B. Wallerstein, M. E. Mogee, and R. A. Schoen (Eds.), *Global dimensions of intellectual property rights in science and technology* (pp. 284–318). Washington, DC: National Academy Press.

Sanders, D. W., and Richardson, M. D. (2002). Whose property is it anyhow? Using electronic media in the academic world. *Journal of Technology Studies, 28*(2), 117–123.

Sanders, D. W., and Shepherd, S. G. (2000). Ethical dilemmas of intellectual property policies at SREB institutions. *Computer Professionals for Social Responsibility (CPSR) Newsletter, 18*(2). Retrieved November 1, 2007, from http://cpsr.org/prevsite/publications/newsletters/issues/2000/Spring2000/sanders-shepard.html/.

Sanger, D. E. (1984, December 18). Campuses fear federal control over research. *New York Times,* B15.

Sanger, D. E. (1985, July 22). Campuses' role in arms debated as "star wars" funds are sought. *New York Times* (Late Edition, East Coast), A1.

Schacht, W. H. (2006). *Patent reform: Issues in the biomedical and software industries.* Washington, DC: Congressional Research Service.

Scott, M. M. (1998, May–June). Intellectual property rights: A ticking time bomb in academia. *Academe, 84*(3), 22–26.

Scully, J. (2004). The virtual professorship: Intellectual property ownership of academic work in a digital era. *McGeorge Law Review, 35,* 227–276.

Seeley, B. E. (2003). Historical patterns in the scholarship of technology transfer. *Comparative Technology Transfer and Society, 1*(1), 7–48.

Seeley, S. L. (2001). Are classroom lectures protected by copyright laws? The case for professors' intellectual property rights. *Syracuse Law Review, 51,* 163–189.

Seymore, S. B. (2006a). How does my work become our work? Dilution of authorship in scientific papers and the need for the academy to obey copyright law. *Richmond Journal of Law and Technology, 12*(3), 1–28.

Seymore, S. B. (2006b). My patent, your patent, or our patent? Inventorship disputes within academic research groups. *Albany Law Journal of Science & Technology, 16,* 125–167.

Shapiro, C. (2000). Navigating the patent thicket: Cross licenses, patent pools, and standard-setting. *Innovation Policy and the Economy, 1,* 119–150.

Shockley, P. (1994). The availability of "trade secret" protection. *Journal of College and University Law, 20,* 309–332.

Simon, T. F. (1983). Faculty writings: Are they "works made for hire" under the 1976 Copyright Act? *Journal of College and University Law, 9*(3), 485–513.

Siwek, S. E. (2007). *The true cost of sound recording piracy to the U.S. economy* (Policy Report no. 188). Lewisville, TX: Institute for Policy Innovation.

Slaughter, S., and Leslie, L. L. (1997). *Academic capitalism: Politics, policies, and the entrepreneurial university.* Baltimore: Johns Hopkins University Press.

Slaughter, S., and Rhoades, G. (1993). Changes in intellectual property statutes and policies at a public university: Revising the terms of professional labor. *Higher Education, 26*(3), 287–312.

Smith, G. K. (1997). Faculty- and graduate student-generated inventions: Is university ownership a legal certainty? *Virginia Journal of Law & Technology, 1,* 21.

Spanier, G., and Sherman, C. H. (2005). Thou shalt not pirate thy neighbor's songs. *Chronicle of Higher Education,* B24.

Springer, A. (2005). *Intellectual property legal issues for faculty and faculty unions.* Washington, DC: American Association of University Professors. Retrieved January 18, 2008, from http://www.aaup.org/NR/exeres/517C85B6-CC13-4A47-AE3E-5C1763713B02.htm.

Stein, D. (Ed.). (2004). *Buying in or selling out? The commercialization of the American research university.* Piscataway, NJ: Rutgers University Press.

Steinbach, S. E. (1989). Photocopying copyrighted course materials: Doesn't anyone remember the NYU case? *Education Law Reporter, 50,* 317–328.

Student Monitor. (2007). *Computing and the Internet: Fall 2006.* Ridgewood, NJ: Student Monitor.

Sun, J. C. (2008). *Academic property: An implied agreement at work.* (Working Paper). Grand Forks, ND: Department of Educational Leadership, University of North Dakota.

Sun, J. C., and Permuth, S. (2007). Evaluations of unionized college and university faculty: A review of the laws. *Journal of Personnel Evaluation in Education, 19*(3–4), 115–134.

Thursby, J. G., and Thursby, M. C. (2002). Who is selling the ivory tower?: Sources of growth in university licensing, *Management Science, 48*(1), 90–104.

Thursby, J. G., and Thursby, M. C. (2003). Industry/university licensing: Characteristics, concerns and issues from the perspective of the buyer. *Journal of Technology Transfer, 28*(3–4), 207–213.

Timiraos, N. (2006, July 6). Free, legal and ignored. *Wall Street Journal,* p. B1.

Todd, J. (2007). Student rights in online course materials: Rethinking the faculty/university dynamic. *Albany Law Journal of Science and Technology, 17,* 311–336.

Townsend, E. (2003). Legal and policy responses to the disappearing "teacher exception," or copyright ownership in the 21st century university. *Minnesota Intellectual Property Review, 4*(2), 209–283.

Trajtenberg, M., Henderson, R., and Jaffe, A. B. (2002). University versus corporate patents: A window on the basics of invention. In A. B. Jaffe and M. Trajtenberg (Eds.), *Patents, citations, and innovations: A window on the knowledge economy* (pp. 51–88). Cambridge, MA: MIT Press.

Troop, D. (2008). New life for casket logos. *Chronicle of Higher Education, 54*(26), A6.

Ubel, F. A. (1994). Who's on first: The trade secret prior user or a subsequent patentee? *Journal of the Patent & Trademark Office Society, 76,* 401–444.

U.S. Copyright Office. (1995). *Reproduction of copyrighted works by educators and librarians.* Circular 21. Washington, DC: U.S. Government Printing Office.

U.S. Patent and Trademark Office (2007). *Manual of patent examining procedure.* Washington, DC: United States Government Printing Office.

von Lohmann, F. (2007). Copyright silliness on campus. *Washington Post,* p. A23.

Wadley, J. B., and Brown, J. M. (1999). Working between the lines of Reid: Teachers, copyrights, work-for-hire and a new Washburn University policy. *Washburn Law Journal, 38,* 385–453.

Wagner, W. (2005). The perils of relying on interested parties to evaluate scientific quality. *American Journal of Public Health, 95*(Supp. 1), S99–S106.

Wallerstein, M. B., Mogee, M. E., and Schoen, R. A. (Eds.). (1993). *Global dimensions of intellectual property rights in science and technology.* Washington, DC: National Academy Press.

Walsh, J. P., Cho, C., and Cohen, W. M. (2005). The view from the bench: Patents, material transfers and biomedical research. *Science, 309*(5743), 2002–2003.

Weidemier, B. J. (2007). Ownership of university inventions: Practical considerations. In A. Krattiger and others (Eds.), *Intellectual property management in health and agricultural innovation: A handbook of best practices* (pp. 495–505). Davis, CA: MIHR-PIPRA.

Welsh, J. F. (2000). Course ownership in a new technological context. *Journal of Higher Education, 71*(6), 668–699.

Wilkinson, M. A. (2000). Copyright in the content of intellectual property: A survey of Canadian university policies. *Intellectual Property Journal, 14,* 141–184.

Woody, R. H., III. (1994). Copyright law and sound recordings. *Music Educators Journal, 80*(6), 29–32.

Yancey, A., and Stewart, C. N., Jr. (2007). Are university researchers at risk for patent infringement? *Nature Biotechnology,* 25.

Zhang, K., and Carr-Chellman, A. A. (2006). Courseware copyright: Whose rights are right? *Journal of Educational Computing Research, 34*(2), 173–186.

Statutes

Copyright Act, 17 U.S.C. §101, et seq. (2008).

Digital Millennium Copyright Act, 17 U.S.C. §1201, et seq. (2008).

Freedom of Information Act, 5 U.S.C. §552, et seq. (2008).

U.S. Patent Act, 35 U.S.C. §101, et. seq. (2008).

Visual Artists Rights Act, 17 U.S.C. §106A (2008).

Cases

A & M Records, Inc. v. *Napster, Inc.,* 114 F.Supp.2d 896 (ND Cal. 2000); 239 F.3d 1004 (9th Cir. 2001).

Apple Computer, Inc. v. *Franklin Computer Corporation,* 714 F.2d 1240 (3rd Cir. 1983).

Applied Innovations, Inc. v. *Regents of the University of Minnesota,* 876 F.2d 626 (8th Cir. 1989).

Baltimore Orioles, Inc. v. *Major League Baseball Players Association,* 805 F.2d 663 (7th circ. 1986)

Basic Books, Inc. v. *Kinko's Graphics Corporation,* 758 F.Supp. 1522 (S.D.N.Y. 1991).

Board of Education v. *American Bioscience, Inc.,* 333 F.3d 1330 (Fed. Cir. 2003).

BV Engineering v. *University of California at Los Angeles,* 858 F.2d 1394 (9th Cir. 1988).

Chavez v. *Arte Publico Press,* 157 F.3d 282 (5th Cir. 2000).

Chou v. *University of Chicago,* 254 F.3d 1347 (Fed. Cir. 2001).

College Savings Bank v. *Florida Prepaid,* 527 U.S. 666 (1999).

Community for Creative Non-Violence v. *Reid,* 490 U.S. 730 (1989).

Diamond v. *Chakrabarty,* 447 U.S. 303 (1980).

Diamond v. *Diehr,* 450 U.S. 175 (1981).

Edmark Industries v. *South Asia International,* 89 F.Supp.2d 840 (E.D. Tex. 2000).

Ex parte Young, 209 U.S. 123 (1908).

Feist Publications, Inc. v. *Rural Telephone Service Company, Inc.,* 499 U.S. 340 (1991).

Fenn v. *Yale University,* 283 F.Supp.2d 615 (D. Conn. 2003).

Florida Prepaid Postsecondary Education Expense Board v. *College Savings Bank,* 527 U.S. 627 (1999).

Foraste v. *Brown University,* 248 F.Supp.2d 71 (D.R.I. 2003).

Genentech v. *Regents of the University of California,* 143 F.3d 1446 (Fed. Cir. 1998).

Gottschalk v. *Benson,* 409 U.S. 63 (1972).

Graham v. *John Deere Co. of Kansas City,* 383 U.S. 1 (1966).

Harper & Row Publishers, Inc. v. *Nation Enterprises,* 471 U.S. 539 (1985).

Hays and MacDonald v. *Sony Corporation of America,* 847 F.2d 412 (7th Cir. 1988).

In re Charter Communications, Inc., 393 F.3d 771 (8th Cir. 2005).

In re Fisher, 421 F.3d 1365 (Fed. Cir. 2005).

In re Hall, 781 F.2d 897 (Fed. Cir. 1986).

Iowa State Univ. Research Foundation, Inc. v. *American Broadcasting Company, Inc.,* 621 F.2d 57 (2d Cir. 1980).

Kawananakoa v. *Polyblank,* 205 U.S. 349 (1907).

Kucharczyk v. *Regents of the University of California,* 946 F.Supp. 1419 (N.D. Cal. 1996).

Madey v. *Duke University,* 307 F.3d 1351 (Fed. Cir. 2002).

M.G.M. Studios, Inc. v. *Grokster,* 545 U.S. 913 (2005).

National Conference of Bar Examiners v. *Multi Legal Studies, Inc.,* 495 F.Supp. 34 (N.D. Ill. 1980).

National Conference of Bar Examiners v. *Multi Legal Studies, Inc.,* 692 F.2d 478 (7th Cir. 1982).

New Star Lasers v. *Regents of the University of California,* 63 F.Supp.2d 1240 (E.D. Cal. 1999).

Princeton Univ. Press v. *Michigan Document Services., Inc.,* 99 F.3d 1381 (6th Cir. 1996) (en banc), cert. denied, 117 S. Ct. 1336 (1997).

Regents of the University of California v. *Eli Lilly and Company,* 119 F.3d 1559 (Fed. Cir. 1997).

Regents of the University of New Mexico v. *Knight,* 321 F.3d 1111 (Fed. Cir. 2003).

Richard Anderson Photography v. *Brown,* 852 F.2d 114 (4th Cir. 1988).

Roth Greeting Cards v. *United Card Company,* 429 F.2d 1106 (9th Cir. 1970).

Salinger v. *Random House, Inc.,* 811 F.2d 90 (2d Cir. 1987).

Seminole Tribe of Florida v. *Florida,* 517 U.S. 44 (1996).

Staggers v. *Real Authentic Sound,* 77 F.Supp.2d 57 (D.D.C. 1999).

State Street Bank and Trust Co. v. *Signature Financial Group,* 149 F.3d 1368 (Fed. Cir. 1998).

Stern v. *Trustees of Columbia University,* 434 F.3d 1375 (Fed. Cir. 2006).

U.S. v. *Board of Trustees of the University of Alabama,* 104 F.3d 1453 (4th Cir. 1997).

University of Rochester v. *G. D. Searle,* 358 F.3d 916 (Fed. Cir. 2004).

University of West Virginia Board of Trustees v. *Vanvoorhies,* 278 F.3d 1288 (Fed. Cir. 2002).

Vas-Cath, Inc. v. *Curators of the University of Missouri,* 473 F.3d 1376 (Fed. Cir. 2007).

Weinstein v. *University of Illinois,* 811 F.2d 1091 (7th Cir. 1987).

Williams v. *Weisser,* 273 Cal.App.2d 726 (Cal. Ct. App. 1969).

Williams Electronics, Inc. v. *Artic Intern., Inc.,* 685 F.2d 870 (3rd Cir. 1982).

Wright v. *Warner Books, Inc.,* 953 F.2d 731 (2d Cir. 1991).

Zomba Enterprises, Inc. v. *Panorama Records, Inc.,* 491 F.3d 574 (6th Cir. 2007).

Name Index

A

Ahrens, F., 49
Aoki, K., 5
Apple, R. D., 84, 85
Arewa, O. B., 17
Ashley, C. L., 42
Audette, L. G., 68
Aufderheide, P., 32, 34, 35
Autry, J. R., 18
Avorn, J., 84, 85, 88

B

Babcock, S., 84
Baez, B., 5, 9
Bagley, M. A., 84, 87
Barnett, A. T., 25, 26
Barton, J. H., 67
Bartow, A., 39
Batista, P. J., 96
Bayh, B., 79
Bearby, S., 94
Belfiore, A., 74
Benjamin, R., 3
Bennett, A. B., 81
Berdahl, R. O., 2
Berger, J. B., 71
Berneman, L., 78
Bhatacharjee, S., 66
Biles, B., 84
Blumenstyk, G., 9, 75, 94, 97, 98, 115
Blumenthal, D., 74, 84, 87, 88, 97
Bobbitt, W. R., 7, 23

Boettiger, S., 81
Bonner, K., 9, 18, 27, 29
Borow, T. A., 21, 22, 27
Bowers, L. J., 68, 69
Boyle, J., 4
Bretschneider, S., 80
Brown, J. M., 21, 23, 96
Bush, V., 78

C

Campbell, E. G., 74, 84, 87, 88
Carlson, S., 49, 50
Carr-Chellman, A. A., 27
Carroll, M. W., 33
Casey, J. J., Jr., 74
Castagnera, J. O., 69, 74
Causino, N., 74, 87, 88
Chavez, D., 105
Chew, P. K., 70
Chmielewski, G., 50
Cho, C., 88
Clarkson, G., 88, 89
Clarridge, B. R., 74
Cohen, W. M., 87, 88
Cottrell, F., 77
Crews, K. D., 4, 32, 34, 36, 39, 41, 42, 45, 109

D

Dai, Y., 80
Daniel, P.T.K., 7, 9, 23, 24
David, P.A., 2, 13, 97, 118

Subject Index

About the Authors

Jeffrey C. Sun is assistant professor of educational leadership and affiliate professor of law at the University of North Dakota. He received his law degree from the Moritz College of Law at The Ohio State University. His research interest is in the area of higher education law, and his work has been published in *Journal of College and University Law, Journal of Personnel Evaluation in Education, Review of Higher Education,* and *Teachers College Record.*

Benjamin Baez is associate professor of higher education in the Department of Educational Leadership and Policy Studies at Florida International University. He received both his law degree and his doctorate in higher education from Syracuse University. He recently published *Affirmative Action, Hate Speech, and Tenure: Narratives About Race, Law, and the Academy.* His teaching and research interests include faculty-employment issues, diversity in higher education, and the law on higher education.

About the ASHE Higher Education Report Series

Since 1983, the ASHE (formerly ASHE-ERIC) Higher Education Report Series has been providing researchers, scholars, and practitioners with timely and substantive information on the critical issues facing higher education. Each monograph presents a definitive analysis of a higher education problem or issue, based on a thorough synthesis of significant literature and institutional experiences. Topics range from planning to diversity and multiculturalism, to performance indicators, to curricular innovations. The mission of the Series is to link the best of higher education research and practice to inform decision making and policy. The reports connect conventional wisdom with research and are designed to help busy individuals keep up with the higher education literature. Authors are scholars and practitioners in the academic community. Each report includes an executive summary, review of the pertinent literature, descriptions of effective educational practices, and a summary of key issues to keep in mind to improve educational policies and practice.

The Series is one of the most peer reviewed in higher education. A National Advisory Board made up of ASHE members reviews proposals. A National Review Board of ASHE scholars and practitioners reviews completed manuscripts. Six monographs are published each year and they are approximately 120 pages in length. The reports are widely disseminated through Jossey-Bass and John Wiley & Sons, and they are available online to subscribing institutions through Wiley InterScience (http://www.interscience.wiley.com).

Call for Proposals

The ASHE Higher Education Report Series is actively looking for proposals. We encourage you to contact one of the editors, Dr. Kelly Ward (kaward@wsu.edu) or Dr. Lisa Wolf-Wendel (lwolf@ku.edu), with your ideas.

Recent Titles

ASHE HIGHER EDUCATION REPORT
Order Form
SUBSCRIPTIONS AND SINGLE ISSUES

DISCOUNTED BACK ISSUES:

Use this form to receive **20% off** *all back issues of ASHE Higher Education Report. All single issues priced at* **$22.40** *(normally $28.00)*

TITLE	ISSUE NO.	ISBN
_____	_____	_____
_____	_____	_____

Call 888-378-2537 *or see mailing instructions below. When calling, mention the promotional code, JB7ND, to receive your discount.*

SUBSCRIPTIONS: *(1 year, 6 issues)*

☐ New Order   ☐ Renewal

U.S.	☐ Individual: $174	☐ Institutional: $228
Canada/Mexico	☐ Individual: $174	☐ Institutional: $288
All Others	☐ Individual: $210	☐ Institutional: $339

Call 888-378-2537 *or see mailing and pricing instructions below. Online subscriptions are available at www.interscience.wiley.com.*

Copy or detach page and send to:
John Wiley & Sons, Journals Dept., 5th Floor
989 Market Street, San Francisco, CA 94103-1741

Order Form can also be faxed to: 888-481-2665

	SHIPPING CHARGES:		
Issue/Subscription Amount: $ _____			
Shipping Amount: $ _____	SURFACE	Domestic	Canadian
(for single issues only—subscription prices include shipping)	First Item	$5.00	$6.00
Total Amount: $ _____	Each Add'l Item	$3.00	$1.50

(No sales tax for U.S. subscriptions. Canadian residents, add GST for subscription orders. Individual rate subscriptions must be paid by personal check or credit card. Individual rate subscriptions may not be resold as library copies.)

☐ Payment enclosed (U.S. check or money order only. All payments must be in U.S. dollars.)

☐ VISA ☐ MC ☐ Amex # _____ Exp. Date _____

Card Holder Name _____ Card Issue # _____

Signature_____ Day Phone _____

☐ Bill Me (U.S. institutional orders only. Purchase order required.)

Purchase order # _____
Federal Tax ID13559302   GST 89102 8052

Name_____

Address _____

Phone _____ E-mail _____

JB7ND

ASHE-ERIC HIGHER EDUCATION REPORT
IS NOW AVAILABLE ONLINE AT WILEY INTERSCIENCE

What is Wiley InterScience?

Wiley InterScience is the dynamic online content service from John Wiley & Sons delivering the full text of over 300 leading scientific, technical, medical, and professional journals, plus major reference works, the acclaimed Current Protocols laboratory manuals, and even the full text of select Wiley print books online.

What are some special features of Wiley InterScience?

Wiley Interscience Alerts is a service that delivers table of contents via e-mail for any journal available on Wiley InterScience as soon as a new issue is published online.
Early View is Wiley's exclusive service presenting individual articles online as soon as they are ready, even before the release of the compiled print issue. These articles are complete, peer-reviewed, and citable.
CrossRef is the innovative multi-publisher reference linking system enabling readers to move seamlessly from a reference in a journal article to the cited publication, typically located on a different server and published by a different publisher.

How can I access Wiley InterScience?

Visit http://www.interscience.wiley.com.

Guest Users can browse Wiley InterScience for unrestricted access to journal Tables of Contents and Article Abstracts, or use the powerful search engine.
Registered Users are provided with a *Personal Home Page* to store and manage customized alerts, searches, and links to favorite journals and articles. Additionally, Registered Users can view free Online Sample Issues and preview selected material from major reference works.
Licensed Customers are entitled to access full-text journal articles in PDF, with select journals also offering full-text HTML.

How do I become an Authorized User?

Authorized Users are individuals authorized by a paying Customer to have access to the journals in Wiley InterScience. For example, a University that subscribes to Wiley journals is considered to be the Customer.

Faculty, staff and students authorized by the University to have access to those journals in Wiley InterScience are Authorized Users. Users should contact their Library for information on which Wiley journals they have access to in Wiley InterScience.

ASK YOUR INSTITUTION ABOUT WILEY INTERSCIENCE TODAY!